CD-ROM
and
Optical Publishing Systems

An assessment of the impact of optical read-only
memory systems on the information industry and
a comparison between them and traditional paper,
microfilm, and online publishing systems.

by
Tony Hendley

BNA 3/18/68

MECKLER PUBLISHING CORPORATION
in association with
CIMTECH/BNBRF

This publication was prepared at Cimtech under a grant from the British National Bibliography Research Fund.

First published in North America by
Meckler Publishing Corporation
11 Ferry Lane West
Westport, CT 06880
ISBN 0-88736-192-7

First published in Great Britain by
Cimtech
The Hatfield Polytechnic
P.O. Box 109
College Lane
Hatfield, Herts AL10 9AB
U.K.

Printed and bound in the United States of America.

CONTENTS

INTRODUCTION 3

1. CD-ROM IN CONTEXT: ITS LINKS WITH OTHER OPTICAL
STORAGE MEDIA 9
1.1 Videodiscs 9
1.2 Compact discs 12
1.2.1 CD-ROMs 13
1.2.2 CD-I 18
1.3 Recordable digital optical disks 26
1.4 Erasable digital optical disks 31

2. STANDARDISATION ISSUES 35

3. STAGES IN THE PRODUCTION OF CD-ROMS 46
3.1 Choice of database 47
3.2 Data capture 48
3.3 Database creation 49
3.4 Data preparation 51
3.5 Pre-mastering 53
3.6 Mastering and replication 53
3.7 What services are available? 53
3.7.1 BRS (Europe) 55
3.7.2 Office Workstations Ltd. 58
3.8 Costs of CD-ROM Production 59

4. WORKSTATION CONFIGURATIONS 61
4.1 Hardware elements of a CD-ROM workstation 61
4.1.1 CD-ROM drives available or under development 63
4.2 Software elements of a CD-ROM workstation 66
4.3 The current position 68
4.3.1 Reference Technology Inc. 70
4.3.2 Digital Equipment Corporation 71
4.4 Future CD-ROM workstations 71

5. APPLICATIONS FOR CD-ROM AS A PUBLISHING MEDIUM 74
5.1 CD-ROM - the solution is coming, now where are
the problems? 74
5.1.1 Trends in computing and publishing 74
5.1.2 Advantages and disadvantages of CD-ROM as a
publishing medium 76
5.2 Defining what we mean by publishing 79
5.3 The professional market 80
5.3.1 In-house publishing 80
5.3.2 Technical publishing 84
5.3.3 Commercial Publishing 87
5.3.3.1 Software distribution 87
5.3.3.2 Graphic databases 89
5.3.3.3 Database publishing 90
5.3.3.4 Specialised information services 98
5.3.3.5 Reference works 100
5.3.3.6 Backfile/collection distribution 101
5.4 The library market 104
5.4.1 Library automation systems 104
5.4.2 Databases and reference material on CD-ROM 106
5.5 The educational market 108
5.6 The domestic market 112

6.	COMPARISON WITH TRADITIONAL PUBLISHING MEDIA	
	AND SYSTEMS	116
6.1	Introduction	116
6.2	Paper	116
6.3	Microfilm	120
6.4	On-line	125
6.5	CD-ROM	128
7.	COMPARISON WITH OTHER OPTICAL PUBLISHING SYSTEMS	133
7.1	OROM	133
7.2	Hybrid videodiscs	135
7.3	Optical cards	136
7.4	Write once optical disks	137
8.	COMPANIES PROVIDING CD-ROM HARDWARE, SERVICES	
	AND SYSTEMS	140
8.1	Drive suppliers	140
8.2.	Data preparers/system integrators	141
9.	PROTOTYPE AND COMMERCIAL CD-ROM PRODUCTS	143
10.	CONCLUSION - THE KEY ISSUES	146

INTRODUCTION

Cimtech (formerly NRCd) have taken an active interest in the potential of optical laser discs for information storage and dissemination ever since Alan Horder's pioneering report 'Videodiscs: their application to information storage and retrieval' published by the Centre in 1979.

In 1985, some six years later, the optical storage industry had grown to the stage where an overall guide to all the many and varied types of discs and their main applications was needed and the Centre published Publication 23 'Videodiscs, compact discs and digital optical disks - an introduction to the technologies and the systems and their potential for information storage, retrieval and dissemination' by Tony Hendley.

In the conclusion to that report we pointed to two promising application areas:

1.   Optical publishing systems, in particular those based on the CD-ROM format

2.   Electronic document storage systems based on recordable digital optical disks.

We promised to follow up the introductory report with two more specific reports which would look in detail at both these areas.

On the publishing side, we felt there was a need for a follow up report which would look in more detail at the standards issues, at the processes involved in the creation of CD-ROM based information products, at the way in which optical publishing systems compared with existing paper, microfilm and online systems and finally, which listed the many companies who are developing hardware and software products in this field and the many information providers who are producing prototype and commercial products based around optical publishing systems.

On the electronic document storage side, we felt there was a need for a more detailed report which would profile some of the application areas where these systems are being installed, analyse the reasons why major companies are investing in the use of these systems and focus on the many optical disk based systems which are now appearing on the market and the many factors which need to be taken into account when evaluating such systems.

'CD-ROM and optical publishing systems - an assessment of the impact of optical read only memory systems on the information industry and a comparison of the new optical publishing systems with traditional paper, microfilm and online publishing systems' (Cimtech Publication 26) is the first of these two reports and the wide range of CD-ROM hardware, software and information products launched in the two years since Publication 23 was published emphasises that we were right to stress the importance of this application area for optical storage systems.

It should be stressed that the main emphasis of this report is on the potential applications of CD-ROM in the commercial and technical publishing arena. Although, clearly, CD-ROM will also have a major role as a pure computer peripheral for the distribution of software and data files to computer users, and in many cases the distinction between publishing and data distribution is hard to draw, our main aim has been to place CD-ROM systems alongside online, microfilm and paper based publishing systems in order to help define its strengths and weaknesses as a publishing medium.

We should also, at the outset, attempt to define exactly what is meant by the phrase 'optical publishing systems' and how they differ from conventional publishing and distribution systems. These differences will help us define the major issues facing potential producers and users of CD-ROM based optical publications.

We shall take a specific, if somewhat simplistic example. Currently, an information provider, such as the British Library or the Library of Congress, who wishes to make available a bibliographic database to several thousand users, has a number of distribution options. We are assuming here that the database has been keyed into a computer system, manipulated, formatted and is held on magnetic disk.

The first distribution channel, if the provider has a sufficiently powerful computer with multiple ports, is to make the database available online. Users would then be able to access it via intelligent terminals/microcomputers linked via a modem and telephone link to the host computer. Alternatively, if the publisher does not have the necessary computer facilities or the resources needed to maintain, administer and market such a service, he can use a host organisation such as DIALOG who will put the database up on their mainframe computer alongside their other databases and make it available to all their existing users. There are now many thousand online databases available throughout the world and the technology and economics of such systems are well documented.

Secondly, the information provider could simply arrange for his database to be output in author/title/classified sequence or any other sequence that meets the search requirements of his potential users, produce print tapes and send these to a Computer Output Microfilm (COM) bureau who will run them on a COM recorder and produce a master copy of the database on microfiche. Copies of the fiche can be produced cheaply using contact duplication processes and distributed to the users who will then need a microfiche reader or reader-printer in order to access the information. The physical size, format and reduction ratio used on the microfiche is governed by national and international standards so the microfiche can be read anywhere in the world.

The third option is, like the second, to produce print tapes but then to output the database onto paper via a laser printer or via a phototypsetter and offset machine. The printed copies of the database can then be distributed to users who do not then require any hardware to access the information.

These are the three main options currently available and, although most information providers actually offer all three, there are advantages and disadvantages to each approach which we discuss in more detail in chapter six. The choice will depend on such factors as the size and complexity of the database, how rapidly the database is updated, how complex the typical user's search requirements are, the value of the information, the cost of the three systems to the information provider and to the end user and the availability of hardware and telecommunications. The same three options exist for publishers of technical material, in-house publishers and even commercial publishers although clearly today, if your main market is the general public there is still a major incentive to use the paper option as it avoids the need for users to purchase and use specialised hardware.

CD-ROM and other read only optical storage media now potentially offer information providers a fourth distribution option.

Currently, read only optical disk systems are being used as publishing media in the consumer environment. Compact discs are being used to publish audio information, in digital form. Copies of records are distributed on CD and played back in hi-fi stack systems and portable CD players. Similarly videodiscs are being used to publish video information in analogue form. Copies of feature films and educational material are distributed on videodisc and played back via a videodisc player linked to a television screen.

CD-ROM (Compact Disc Read Only Memory) is being and will be used to publish/distribute digital data (data, text, graphics, etc.) and the minimum configuration required for the user to access that data is a CD-ROM drive linked to a microcomputer. In the example given above, the bibliographic database would be organised and formatted for distribution on CD-ROM, magnetic tapes containing the formatted database would be sent to a mastering facility, a master CD-ROM database would be created and replicated CD-ROMs stamped out and sent to end users who would load them onto their CD-ROM drive and access the data via a micro or minicomputer.

In many respects, therefore, CD-ROM publishing systems are closer to online distribution systems than to microform or paper systems. Certainly the end user needs a computer to access the information and the information is held in digital form and can be manipulated and searched interactively. Also, for database publishing the software used to create and search online databases will be adapted and used to create and access CD-ROM databases. However, with CD-ROM systems the actual database is sent to the user for access locally and in this respect the systems are more akin to microfilm and paper publishing systems.

Furthermore, just because CD-ROM publications need to be accessed via a computer system, it does not necessarily mean that in future they are limited in application to the distribution of complex databases and files of raw data to professional computer users. With the continuing reduction in price of computer systems and the development of simple user friendly software systems, many of the advocates of CD-ROM publishing point to the fact that within five years PCs with integral CD-ROM drives could be available for £500 or less - little more than the cost of a microfiche system when consumable costs are added to the price of a fiche reader and CD-ROM could begin to challenge microfilm and paper as a generic publishing medium for distributing a wide range of information from technical manuals and directories to encyclopedias, and dictionaries. Philips/Sony's newly announced CD-I system, which we describe in detail in Chapter One, is one example of how, in the future, for the consumer and education market, a combined CD-ROM drive and computer system could be made available at a low price for use by people with no knowledge of computing systems at all.

Even this brief outline should serve to indicate that CD and other such optical publishing systems pose a number of significant issues, issues which fall into two categories. The first category relates to CD-ROM as a computer peripheral: which interfaces exist between CD-ROM drives and computer systems, what performance is offered by CD-ROM media and what logical format is required to allow data stored on a CD-ROM to be read by multiple computer systems running multiple operating systems. The second category relates to CD-ROM as a publishing medium: what are the mastering and replication costs, what turnaround times can be expected, how easy will it be to search the contents of a CD-ROM, what speed of retrieval will be offered, how many versions of a CD-ROM database will have to be produced to reach all potential users, what software will be needed to provide access to the database and what is the installed base of CD-ROM drives likely to be?

Perhaps the key issue which many publishers are looking into is will CD-ROM ever become a generic publishing medium like paper and microfilm. Given the fierce competition in the computer industry and the rapidly evolving PC market, what level of stability can publishers build on in a publishing system based on a computer peripheral?

Each chapter of this report is devoted to dealing with one of the main issues relating to CD-ROM and while we cannot claim to resolve them all in a report of this nature we can, at least, attempt to identify the main ones which have to be considered from the standpoint of both the information provider and the end user.

Chapter One aims to place CD-ROM in context by relating it to the other optical media currently on the market or under development - videodisc, compact disc, recordable digital optical disk and erasable digital optical disk systems - which all make use of the same technology but are aimed at different applications. We do not aim to provide an exhaustive technical account of all the different types of disks and the physical processes involved in recording data onto and reading data back from them as these were covered in detail in Publication 23 and users new to this subject are referred back to that report as an introduction to the technology. All we have done here is draw on some of the material prepared for that report in order to provide a simplified guide to the technology and update it by covering new developments such as CD-I.

Chapter Two outlines the areas where standardisation is a major issue and looks at the efforts being made to introduce standards.

Chapter Three identifies all the major stages involved in producing a CD-ROM to give publishers and other prospective users a perspective on all the processes involved, the decisions to be made and the advantages and limitations which result.

Chapter Four looks at the hardware and software required to playback CD-ROM systems and considers cost, ergonomic and marketing factors which will need to be taken into account by publishers and users of these systems.

Chapter Five looks at the key application areas where CD-ROM systems will and could be used, both in the consumer and the commercial field.

Chapter Six compares CD-ROM with existing paper, microfilm and online distribution systems.

Chapter Seven compares CD-ROMs with other optical publishing media - OROM, hybrid videodiscs, optical cards and recordable optical disks.

Chapter Eight attempts to give a snapshot of the current state of play, listing companies involved in the supply of hardware, software and CD-ROM data preparation services.

Chapter Nine describes some of the many commercial and prototype CD-ROM products which have either been launched or are currently under development.

Chapter Ten concludes by looking at the key issues posed by CD-ROM and optical publishing systems.

1. CD ROM IN CONTEXT: ITS LINKS WITH OTHER OPTICAL STORAGE MEDIA

CD-ROM (Compact Disc Read Only Memory) is one of a large number of laser optical storage devices which have been leaving the laboratories since the early 1970's and moving into the marketplace. In chronological terms, the first read only optical storage product to reach the market was the videodisc in 1978 which was followed by the Compact Audio Disc in 1982 and the CD-ROM in 1985. In order to place CD-ROM in context and demonstrate how it is related to these other optical read only media, we give a brief account of the processes involved in producing both videodiscs and compact audio discs before going on to concentrate on CD-ROMs. To complete the picture, we conclude the section with a brief account of recordable and erasable digital optical disks.

1.1 Videodiscs

Videodiscs were primarily developed by consumer electronic companies to compete with video cassette recorders (VCRs) for a share of the lucrative consumer market for video recording and playback systems. It was felt that they would compete with VCRs in just the same way that gramophone records compete with audio cassette systems. Advantages claimed for the videodisc systems were that disc replication costs were low and hence the discs would be cheap to buy, the players would be cheaper than VCR's, the image quality offered by videodiscs would be superior to cassettes, there would be far less wear during playback and the videodisc systems would be far more flexible, offering facilities such as freeze-frame, random access and slow speed forward and reverse.

In practice, the lack of a record facility prevented videodiscs taking off as a consumer item but the many extra features available with videodisc systems made them very attractive to the institutional market where they are being widely used for interactive training and point of sale systems.

In the early 1970's two companies - Philips in Europe and MCA (Music Corporation of America) in the U.S.A. - demonstrated optical videodisc systems that shared many common features. The Philips system was called VLP (video long playing) and the MCA system 'Discovision'. In 1974 it was announced that, in the consumer market, the two systems were to merge, with Philips manufacturing and marketing hardware worldwide and MCA joining Philips in software production and distribution. The system was finally brought to the market in the U.S. in late 1978. Since then Discovision have pulled out of the market and their place has been taken by Pioneer who also manufacture their own brand of players. Philips have gone on to perfect their own disc replication process, establish their own replication facilities and launch a complete range of videodisc players under the brand name of Laservision.

The Laservision system established a de facto standard for videodisc mastering which is now widely observed. The programme information, which can be stored on film or tape, is read by a helical scan videotape unit and used to modulate the intensity of a laser beam which is focused on a rotating glass master disc which is coated with a thin film of positive photoresist. Once recording is complete the exposed areas of photoresist are etched away to leave a master disc containing video information encoded in its periodicity and length as pits. The master's recording surface is then metallised using an evaporated metal coating and becomes the source for generating identical submasters.

There are then two main processes used for the mass production of replicate discs. Philips and 3M use a cold photopolymerisation process referred to as 2P while Pioneer, Sony and others make use of a compression injection moulding technique. Both these replication methods involve the pressing or stamping of discs and hence are closely allied to gramophone record production techniques and the same economics apply - the more copies produced the cheaper they are.

Both the mastering and the replication equipment is extremely sophisticated and hence expensive to install and both mastering and replication must be conducted in top clean room conditions so for the foreseeable future videodisc mastering and replication will not be an in-house operation for publishers, it will be carried out by vendors of videodisc systems and specialist media producers such as 3M, Philips/Polygram and Pioneer.

While the replication techniques vary slightly, all laser optical videodisc systems currently on the market make use of the same basic playback technique which involves using a low power laser as a stylus and a photo-detector to collect light reflected by a disc. Such systems are, not surprisingly, called reflective systems. The videodisc players currently on the market range in price from approximately £400 for serial play consumer products up to over £2,000 for units with their own internal microprocessor which can be programmed to retrieve and display a sequence of frames in a predetermined order and which can be linked to and controlled by external computer systems.

These so called non-contact optical videodisc systems offer a number of significant advantages in terms of both playback facilities and durability over older capacitive videodisc systems and other media such as serial play video cassette systems which recommend the optical videodisc systems for use in computer based training systems and interactive point of sale and other visual information systems.

Firstly, the laser pick-up device can be moved at random across the disc and will operate at a range of different speeds or in still-frame mode. Secondly, as there is no stylus in contact with the disc there is no likelihood of wear either in normal usage or when freeze-frame facilities are required. Thirdly, since the laser used to read the information on the disc can be focused with extreme accuracy, it is possible to set the laser beam to ignore the protective coating on the outside of the disc and focus straight on to the recorded information contained within the disc. This means that dust and scratches on the protective covering of the disc do not result in a loss of picture quality.

The Laservision videodiscs have a diameter of 12 inches and the information is encoded on the disc as a series of pits which vary in length and spacing, arranged on a spiral track. A single track of pits or flats contains all the information necessary for a colour video programme with stereo sound or two separate sound channels (if bilingual operation is required) plus control data for playback operations. There are some 54,000 tracks per disc side and the disc rotates at 1,800 rpm for U.S. 60Hz 525 line systems and 1,500 rpm for European 50Hz 625 line systems. With one frame recorded on each track this provides a playing time of 30 minutes per disc side. The information on the disc is read by pointing a laser beam onto the underside of the disc and focusing it directly into the bottom of the pits. The light is then diffracted and reflected back through servo-tracking mirrors to a photodiode.

During playback of a disc, tracking of the read head proceeds from the innermost to the outermost track. The discs can be configured to offer a choice of two playback modes designed to cater for the needs of two different markets.

With Constant Angular Velocity (CAV) or active play mode, one frame is recorded on each track and the disc rotates at constant velocity so the linear tracking velocity increases from the innermost track where it is least to the outermost track where it is greatest. As each track holds one frame, a single frame can be frozen on the screen by directing the read head to scan one track continuously. Similarly the speed and direction of the pick-up device can be exactly controlled and each frame on the disc, up to 54,000, can be numbered and the read head directed to go to and read any one in a fraction of a second.

CAV mode is therefore the ideal mode for use in interactive videodisc systems where individual frames need to be called up and displayed to answer specific enquiries or as part of a computer based training system.

In the consumer market, however, where the main requirement was simply for serial replay of feature films, CAV mode, with one frame per track, represented a poor use of space and restricted the playing time available on each side of the disc to 30 minutes of video. Hence, for the consumer market, Philips abandoned the principle of one frame per revolution of the disc and varied the velocity of the disc to provide Constant Linear Velocity (CLV) mode or long play discs. Using CLV mode, the playing time of each side of the disc can be expanded as on the outer tracks of the disc with a large circumference, two or three frames can be recorded. Using this recording technique and varying the speed of rotation of the disc at the playback stage the playing time can be expanded from 30 minutes to 60 minutes per side. The trade off, however, is that individual frames cannot easily be accessed on a track by track basis and the freeze-frame facilities are sacrificed.

Clearly, from the publishing viewpoint, CAV discs with the fast random access facilities show the most promise. Indeed a number of companies such as Laserdata, TMS, Reference Technology and Philips with their Laservision ROM, have devised techniques for encoding digital data within the video signal of the videodisc so the vast storage capacity and random access facilities provided by the videodisc can be used to distribute digital databases in a number of electronic publishing applications.

These systems are often referred to as hybrid discs because it is possible to intermix digital data, video and audio information on the same videodisc side and if the whole of a 12 inch videodisc is used to store data the capacity is extremely high. Digital data can be impressed on the lines of a composite video frame as well as analogue video signals and in theory some 400 bits can be written on each TV line so with approximately 500 lines per frame and 50,000 frames per side there is a theoretical storage capacity of 1 Gbyte per side. Philips, with their Laservision ROM are able to store the full 54,000 video frames plus over 300 Mbytes of digital data in tracks normally reserved for audio information.

The disadvantage with hybrid disc systems as a vehicle for publishing information at present is the lack of standardisation and the high cost of the hardware. At present hybrid discs produced by TMS, Reference Technology or Philips have to be read on those companies' own drives because the encoding technique is proprietary to each of them. In addition the minimum hardware requirement is an industrial videodisc player, a controller/decoder card for a PC and an IBM PC and the price tag for that is £4,000-5,000.

1.2 Compact Discs

In chronological terms, compact discs (CDs) were later on the market than optical videodiscs. Optical videodiscs were first shown in 1973 and became commercially available in the U.S. in 1978. Compact discs were first shown in 1980 and were launched commercially in 1983. However, sales of compact disc players to the consumer market have already outstripped sales of videodisc players in what has been described as one of the most successful launches of a consumer electronic product with several million players sold in the first two years of its launch.

Whereas optical videodiscs were originally intended to compete with video cassette recorders for a share of the consumer video playback market, compact discs compete with gramophone records for a share of the audio playback market.

Compact disc systems are all standardised on the format and digital recording techniques designed by Philips and the error detection and correction systems jointly developed by Philips and Sony. These are embodied in what is known as the Philips and Sony 'Red Book' which is made available, on the payment of a small fee, to companies who wish to have a licence to produce discs or drives that meet the standard. The main aim of the standard is to achieve total compatibility so all CDs produced to the standard can be played on all CD players designed to meet the standard. It is this compatibility which has led to CD's success in the consumer marketplace.

The physical processes involved in producing a compact disc are virtually identical to those described above for a videodisc except that the material recorded on the disc is in a different format and the master and replicate discs are single sided with a 12 cm or 4.72 inch diameter rather than a 12 inch diameter.

Production of a compact disc is a three stage process comprising premastering, mastering and replication of the discs. At the premastering stage audio information is recorded onto digital tape to provide a standard input to the mastering process. At the mastering stage the audio information stored on tape is recorded onto a glass master compact disc using a laser beam. The replication stage involves the creation of a number of sub-masters from the master CD and the production of large volumes of replicate discs from these sub-masters.

The key difference between CDs and videodiscs, other than their size, is that the audio information is stored on the CDs in digital form so CDs are a digital storage medium while videodiscs are essentially an analogue storage medium. With CDs the audio information is digitally encoded prior to storage on the discs and is read off the discs as a bit stream at rates in excess of 4 Mbits per second. At the output stage the digital information on the CDs is passed through a digital to analogue converter for output as a series of audio signals which can then be replayed on standard consumer high fidelity systems making use of the same amplifier and loudspeaker systems as would be used to replay the signals picked up from a record or cassette deck.

For compact disc replication the basic raw material used is a polycarbonate called macrolon which is liquidised and injected under high pressure and heat into the injection moulding machines. After moulding, the single disc surface which carries the pits is coated with a thin layer of aluminium to produce a reflecting surface for the laser beam. The surface itself is coated with a protective lacquer which is dripped on the rotating disc and before labelling and packaging the disc is centred and the centre hole punched in.

Like analogue records, compact discs are produced with a run-in section, a music section and a run-out section, all of which contain information in digital coded form. In the run-in section CDs have a table of contents and details of the number of recorded tracks and the time from the start of the disc to each track. Data is recorded onto each CD master in a spiral of tracks starting at the inside of the disc and working outwards and there is provision for dividing each CD into a maximum of 99 tracks. The standard 12 cm disc contains some 20,000 spirals in the programme area and in these are recorded a series of laser cut pits. Using this recording technique one 12 cm CD can store over 60 minutes of high quality stereo which, when error correction and detection codes are taken into account, represents a storage capacity of 7 Gbits.

Playback of the discs in a CD player involves the use of a laser optical system which has to be accurately positioned over the relevant track on the disc and accurately focused on the disc's recorded surface. The CD players use the same reflective system as the videodiscs to read the data from the discs. A low power laser beam is shone onto the disc's recorded surface and the intensity of the reflected laser beam is less when the laser reads a pit than when the laser reads a land (the area of the coating which has not been etched away). The different intensities of reflected light are detected by photocells and constitute the raw digital signal.

The discs are played back at a Constant Linear Velocity (CLV) of 1.25m/sec from the inside to the outside which means that the rotational speed varies from 430 to 200 rpm. CLV mode is employed to maximise the storage capacity and hence the playing time but it does mean that access is slower than with CAV discs. In practice a particular piece of music on the disc is accessed not via its track number (1-99) but by its position on the disc spiral counted in terms of the time it takes to reach it in normal playback from the beginning of the disc. This is not a significant limitation when storing audio information but it does limit the applications for CDs as a computer storage peripheral (see next section on CD-ROM). The final significant point to make about CDs is that since they are a digital medium, they are supplied with a sophisticated error detection and correction system devised by Philips and Sony which serves as the basis for the error detection and correction system used on CD-ROMs.

1.2.1 CD-ROMs (Compact Disc Read Only Memories)

In the section above on videodiscs we described how an analogue consumer product had been adapted and used by a number of companies to develop information delivery systems based on hybrid videodiscs. It was not surprising, therefore, that when a digital consumer product - the compact disc - was introduced, computer hardware manufacturers, software suppliers, publishers and database providers also took a considerable interest in the potential of this new medium as a computer storage peripheral and an electronic publishing medium.

The result was that, within two years of the launch of the first commercial CD audio player and the availability of the 'Red Book' standard, Philips showed a CD-ROM (Read Only Memory) player which was, in essence, a direct adaptation of the CD system for publishing and data processing applications. The worldwide 'Red Book' standard which had initially been established for CD audio was extended in the CD-ROM 'Yellow Book' standard to cover the requirements of the data processing environment so the new CD-ROM drives and discs could benefit from the use of proven technologies.

Before describing the differences in CD-ROM and CD formats, we must stress the similarities. They are both mass produced using the same physical mastering and replication processes and plants designed to master and replicate CDs and can be easily adapted to master and replicate CD-ROMs. The discs have the same physical dimensions - diameter, thickness and chemical composition. The CD-ROM drives rotate at the same speed as the CD players and both CD and CD-ROM discs are recorded and read in Constant Linear Velocity (CLV) mode. The CD-ROM drives and CD players use the same modulation systems and error detection and correction systems which are defined in the Red and Yellow books as EFM (eight to fourteen modulation) and CIRC (cross interleaved reed solomon coding).

However, CD-ROMs, as we have stated above, are primarily designed to store digital data whereas CDs were designed to store digitally encoded audio information. The result is that the CD-ROM 'Yellow Book' standard has made provision for more accurate addressing of data and for an extra level of error detection.

Both CDs and CD-ROMs use the same basic control and display (subcoding) systems for locating/addressing information. As we have seen above, the subcoding system for CDs and CD-ROMs divides the disc into three parts: the lead-in area, the programme area and the lead-out area. With CDs and CD-ROMs the programme area can be divided into a maximum of 99 tracks or programmes. For CDs storing only digitally encoded audio information, this is sufficient to enable any section of audio to be addressed quickly.

With CD-ROM, as defined in the Yellow Book, such a division is not sufficient and there is a need to add in a facility to access specific data more precisely and to provide for extra error correction. Hence, in the Yellow Book provision is made for every one of the 99 tracks or programmes to contain either digitally encoded audio information or pure computer data. The two types of information are handled in different ways and are referred to as two different modes. In practice most CD-ROMs currently being produced contain just one data programme but the standard will support mixed mode discs holding both pure computer data and digitally encoded audio and in future a range of other types of information, each defined as a further mode.

The error detection and correction (EDAC) specified in the Red Book standard is adequate for storing audio information where one lost bit will not affect the sound reproduction and data, to quote Philips, tends to degrade gracefully, but would not be adequate for storing pure digital data where, to quote Philips again, one uncorrected bit error could mean the difference between a plus or a minus sign in your bank balance. The result is that CD-ROM drives require a further level of error detection and correction than compact disc players.

To achieve this, the CD-ROM 'Yellow Book' standard divides the data programmes on a CD-ROM into logical units - 2 Kbyte data blocks - one of which is stored in each physical sector on the CD-ROM. Each sector on the CD-ROM disc actually contains some 98 CD frames, each of 24 bytes, to give a total sector capacity of 2,352 bytes of data of which 2,048 bytes are always for user data and the remaining 304 bytes are used for data which the drives need to locate data on the disc, additional error correction systems or additional user data, as illustrated below:

Sync field	12 bytes
Header field	4 bytes
User data field	2,048 bytes
Auxiliary data field	288 bytes
Total	2,352 bytes

All data in a block, except those in the synchronisation field, are scrambled. A mode byte then describes the nature of the user data.

At present, in the Yellow Book standard, Mode 1 is defined for computer data storage where, as explained above, the additional error correction is required and hence the 288 bytes in the auxiliary data field are used for another level of error correction.

However, the CD-ROM standard also makes provision for other information to be stored on the disc - information which will degrade gracefully, and where, as we have stated above, the existing EDAC system specified in the Red Book is adequate. A second mode is therefore defined (Mode 2) where the 288 bytes in the auxiliary data field is used to store more information rather than any additional levels of error correction.

The result is that in future the same basic CD-ROM drive could be used for both audio playback and data retrieval and already a number of combined audio/data CD-ROM players have been shown, aimed at the domestic market where they could be linked to personal computer and rack hi-fi systems. The combined players would have two outputs. In the case of the audio CD the output goes via a digital to analogue converter and from there to an amplifier and loudspeaker system. In the case of CD-ROM the digital data on the disc is sent to a computer or an output device such as a monitor or a printer.

Looking at CD-ROM production, we have pointed out above that the disc mastering and production facilities which are already well established for the CD audio systems, can be used to produce CD-ROMs as well. The only process that differs is the data preparation/premastering required to produce the master tape.

The effort involved at the data preparation stage will depend on a number of factors such as whether the data is already in machine readable form, how it is to be presented on the screen and what retrieval software is required. We deal with this aspect of CD-ROM production in more detail in Chapter Three. Basically, if a CD-ROM is being used to distribute a database, the database has to be organised, indexed and formatted by a data preparation facility and suitably formatted magnetic tapes sent to a mastering facility where the tapes carrying the customer's database, divided into 2Kbyte blocks, are processed in order to add the necessary synchronisation patterns, headers (address and mode indicators) plus error detection and correction codes required to form CD-ROM sectors. During recording the information is encoded into the CD format and the process follows as for the CD audio.

We have already made the point that the CD audio contains up to 99 audio tracks and these can be replaced by the same number of data tracks when, for retrieval, the user simply selects the track and number of bytes required. Alternatively, since the whole 600 Mbytes are in one continuous stream, it is possible to select a particular byte number to start and the following n bytes. Since CD-ROM data are organised sequentially along a spiral and are read with CLV, they are addressed in absolute time. The total time is that required to read the data sequentially and this is divided into 0 to 60 minutes, 0 to 59 seconds and 0 to 74 fractions of a second. A microprocessor can then interpret these time instructions via a simple time/position algorithm to give random access.

CD-ROMs, like CDs, are single sided 12cm diameter discs and the total user storage capacity is 550 Mbytes (formatted). This compares very favourably with other storage devices for personal computers including flexible diskettes with storage capacities of 0.5-1.5 Mbytes, hard disks with capacities up to 70 Mbytes and magnetic tapes with capacities up to 200 Mbytes.

However, CD-ROM is a read only medium and is therefore not intended to replace any of the above storage media but rather to supply PC users and indeed minicomputer and mainframe computer users with a low cost, high capacity, static data distribution medium and hence can be loosely defined as an optical publishing medium.

We deal with the question of CD-ROM standards in detail in Chapter Two but we must give a brief outline of the current position here. When dealing with CDs we stated that the Red Book standard ensured that all CDs could be played on all CD players. Physically, this is true with CD-ROMs too - any CD-ROM produced to the Yellow Book standard will fit in any CD-ROM drive and can be read but because CD-ROM drives are computer peripherals and users need a computer to access the data stored on the CD-ROM, a number of other factors militate against compatibility.

The first of these is the volume and file structures used on the CD-ROM discs or, in other words, how the data is organised logically on the disc. The Yellow Book standard does not address this issue because it is directly linked to the computer and operating system environment where the CD-ROM is likely to be used. Hence for CD-ROMs to be readable on a range of computer systems by a range of operating systems, there is a need to define a CD-ROM volume and file structure standard.

A Group called the High Sierra Group in the U.S. have attempted to cater for this requirement by producing a 'Working Paper for Information Processing - Volume and File Structure of Compact Read Only Optical Discs for Information Interchange' and we describe the main points and implications for the publishing industry in Chapter Two.

The second issue relates to the CD-ROM drives. Drives have different controllers and the commands which the controllers accept and the format in which they must be supplied are not standardised across manufacturers. Then there is the physical/logical connection between the host microcomputer and the controller. This is another area where, once the file structure standard is adopted, de facto standards will need to be worked out between drive manufacturers and computer manufacturers/operating system suppliers. We cover this area in more detail in Chapter Four on workstation configurations.

The third issue relates to the choice of retrieval software. If a publisher wishes to provide free text retrieval facilities - an almost essential requirement when dealing with 550 Mbytes of data and trying to access it on a PC - then he has to choose a retrieval software supplier such as BRS, Harwell or Battelle and then organise his data according to the requirements of that supplier. In addition he will have to supply versions of that retrieval software package with the database, either on the CD-ROM itself or on a separate floppy disk and that fact will immediately limit the range of computer/operating systems that the CD-ROM database can be used on. The limiting factors will be how many versions of the software package there are, which operating systems they run on and what is the minimum RAM and magnetic disk storage required on the PC to support the software.

Suffice it to say at this stage that compatibility of CD-ROM systems is a far more complex issue than compatibility of CD discs and players due to the fact that CD-ROM drives are computer peripherals.

The first drives to be shown - the Philips CM 100 and the Hitachi CDR 1502S - are simply modified consumer CD players. They are relatively bulky units and are designed as standalone units which will sit on top of the PC's CPU, below the monitor or alongside the PC. Other more compact 5.25 inch CD-ROM drives are becoming available such as the Hitachi CDR 2500 and we are promised half height 5.25 inch drives which will fit into the form slide of a PC, replacing the flexible diskette drive, and will make use of the PC's internal power supply.

Due to the use of the CLV mode, average access times on a CD-ROM are relatively slow when compared with magnetic disks.

The Philips CM 100 offers a storage capacity of 600 Mbytes (unformatted), average access times of 1 second and maximum access times of 2 seconds for each seek. The data transfer rate from the CD-ROM drive to the PC is 1.41 Mbits/sec using a proprietary high speed serial interface. The standalone drive measures 115mm (h) x 320mm (w) x 267mm (d) and weighs approximately 5 kg.

The Hitachi CDR 1502S offers a storage capacity of 552 Mbytes (formatted), average access times of 0.5 seconds and maximum access times of 1 second for each seek. The data transfer rate from the CD-ROM drive to the PC is 1.41 Mbits/sec (nominal), 1.22 Mbits/sec (minimum). The standalone drive measures 85mm (h) x 435mm (w) x 289mm (d) and weighs approximately 5.9 kg.

The Hitachi CDR 2500 built-in type CD-ROM offers exactly the same specifications as the CDR 1502S but measures 83mm (h) x 146mm (h) x 203mm (d) and weighs about 3 kg.

Currently, Philips use their Polygram plant in Germany and their Blackburn plant in England to master and replicate the discs. In theory, all the companies who are mastering and replicating CDs could apply for a licence from Philips/Sony to also produce CD-ROMs so there should be no shortage of capacity when usage of CD-ROM systems takes off. In addition to Polygram in Europe there are already a number of CD-ROM mastering and replicating facilities in the U.S. and Japan with 3M, Sony and Hitachi-Denon prominent among the list of companies able to offer such services.

Currently the cost of mastering one CD-ROM (assuming that the data is already available on tape in the required format) is approximately ₤2,200 and the cost of replicating the discs is ₤12-18 per disc, depending on whether a run of hundreds or thousands is required. In future, as capacity increases, experts predict that the mastering costs will drop to roughly ₤1,000 per master and ₤1 per replicate in high volume. Turnaround times from delivery of final formatted tape to despatch of replicate discs is 2-3 weeks but again, as capacity grows, turnaround times of 1 week or less (depending on the number of replicates required) are anticipated.

There will be a major requirement for service houses capable of providing a full premastering service and, in many cases, a database creation or conversion service for companies who wish to develop information services for distribution on CD-ROM either in-house or commercially and we look at some of the factors involved in database preparation and premastering in Chapter Three.

1.2.2 CD-I (Compact Disc Interactive)

Before leaving compact discs altogether, we must describe the much publicised CD-I (Compact Disc Interactive) specification. On 24th February, 1986, Philips and Sony announced plans for the CD Interactive Media (CD-I) specification. It was a rushed announcement to meet the timetable of the Microsoft Conference and it led to considerable confusion in the marketplace with people seeing it as an alternative to CD-ROM or a development of CD audio. In effect, CD-I represents a logical development of the CD-ROM Yellow Book standard and, as indicated above, is one of many such developments which are provided for within the standard.

The best commentary on CD-I and its relationship to CD and CD-ROM systems we have read was provided by Knowledgeset Corporation in an open letter to the optical publishing industry on CD-ROM and CD-I standard issues and we include extracts from it here.

Philips and Sony have taken the lead, over the past six years, in defining standards for Compact Disc music and data storage. The 'Red Book' covers CD digital audio recording standards and is well known and widely accepted.

The 'Yellow Book', as described above, gives physical recording standards for CD-ROM and added error detection and correction coding to meet the demands of data storage and retrieval. It too is well understood and widely accepted.

Philips and Sony have now announced plans for a third standard – the Green Book – which defines CD Interactive (CD-I).

The Red Book and Yellow Book applications do not basically overlap – there is no confusion about these standards. However, CD-ROM and CD-I both have applications in data processing and this has led to confusion about their respective roles.

The CD-ROM standard is the basis for CD-I. CD-ROM is not outmoded in any way by CD-I. CD-I is not a superset of CD-ROM. Instead it is a special use of CD-ROM that has a number of important components. Special use means that the CD-ROM data records can contain data in specific formats which include: sixteen kinds of audio, two video resolutions, one microprocessor object code and one file system.

CD-ROM is the foundation of all compact disc data format standards. These are like a tree where the trunk is CD-ROM and the branches, like CD-I and other new versions to follow, are all application specific. CD-I, as defined by Philips and Sony, is the consumer entertainment and education branch and attempts to meet all the requirements of that marketplace. The High Sierra Group proposed standard could be regarded as CD-C for CD commercial – aiming to meet commercial data processing requirements.

In summary, the CD-I recording format is identical to CD-ROM. CD-I simply gives the user some standard ways in which to represent common forms of information that they can use when the forms are appropriate for their application.

CD-I also attempts to define a complete system because it is aimed at the consumer market and the requirement there is seen to be for an appliance which provides a particular function or set of functions and which is as simple to use as a record player or CD player. CD-I has to be a simple system and hence, while CD-I is logically an extension of the CD-ROM standard, conceptually, CD-I also represents an extension of the CD digital audio concept of a consumer product offering total compatibility of discs and players by defining both the way in which information is recorded on the disc and the equipment needed to read the disc.

With CD-I, therefore, as with CD, Philips and Sony have defined not only the medium but also the equipment that will be needed to read it, the audio processes, the video processes, the choice of microprocessor and the operating system so that they can achieve their goal of being able to play all CD-I discs on all CD-I players.

In addition, because, CD-I players will be used in the home, it is a requirement that CD audio discs can be played on CD-I players too. It is also expected, and claimed by Philips, that following the work of the High Sierra Group, data recorded on CD-ROM according to the provisions made by the HSG working standard would also potentially be readable on a CD-I player.

Certainly Philips are committed to using the volume and file structures defined by the HSG working standard in their CD-I discs. However, for a database on CD-ROM to be usable on CD-I then the software vendor would need to have developed his software specifically to run on the CD-I player and use the CD-I player's operating system and, although this could potentially be done in the future, very little standard retrieval software - particularly free text retrieval software, would be able to run on the CD-I player.

In effect, therefore, while CD-I is still a computer peripheral and a computer interface to link a CD-I player to other computer systems will be available, a computer itself will be incorporated in the CD-I player so there will be no need to attach a CD-I player to a computer system to access the data. All that is required will be to link the CD-I player to a standard televison or monitor and control it via a keypad or mouse device. The CD-I player will not have any magnetic disk drives so all the information - including the application programme, the additional information needed for the operating system and all the data must be on the CD-I disc itself as that will be the only medium used to run the complete application.

We must now look in more detail at the CD-I specifications.

CD-I is a complete, self-contained specification based on three basic requirements outlined above - full compatibility of CD-I discs and CD-I players, the requirement that CD-I should be a single media system and the requirement that CD-I must be based on and piggy back on existing mass-produced consumer electronic products (CDs and television).

Philips are targeting five main application areas with CD-I:

1. In the car
        Maps
        Navigation systems
        Diagnostics

2. Education and training
        Do-it-yourself
        Training
        Reference works
        Talking books

3. Entertainment
        Music plus visuals
        Action games
        Animations
        Activity simulation

4. Creative leisure
        Filming
        Drawing/painting
        Composing

5. Work at home
        Document processing
        Information retrieval

The above application areas helped define the requirements made of CD-I. Many of the above applications imply real-time dependencies between audio and visual data and hence lead to a requirement for physical interleaving. In addition, it is obvious that with CD-I there will be a need to handle two forms of data, data which degrades gracefully (audio and uncompressed video) and data that is either there or not (such as text and data) where error rates are crucial. In the former case, maximum bandwidth is the key requirement so images can be refreshed, in the latter case an extra level of error detection and correction is required.

These functional requirements determined how data was formatted on CD-I.

We start with the basic CD-ROM sector defined as follows:

2,352 bytes

12 bytes Sync field	4 bytes Header field	2,048 bytes User data	288 bytes Auxiliary data

CD-I is based on Mode 2 where the auxiliary data field is used to store more user data - audio/visual:

2,352 bytes

12 bytes Sync field	4 bytes Header field	2,336 bytes User data

In order to meet the requirement for real-time physical interleaving of data, a sub-header mechanism is defined as follows:

2,352 bytes

12 bytes Sync field	4 bytes Header	8 bytes Sub-header	2,328 bytes User data

In addition, to cater for the two forms of data which CD-I is designed to handle, with two levels of data integrity, two physical formats are defined in the specification. The first of the two formats, catering for data form 1 - text and computer data - uses the additional error detection and correction defined in CD-ROM Mode 1. The second of the two formats, catering for data form 2 - real-time audio and visual data - aims to provide maximum bandwidth.

FORM 1 (EDC/ECC)
2,352 bytes

12 bytes Sync	4 bytes Header	8 bytes Sub-header	2,048 bytes User data	280 bytes EDC/ECC

FORM 2 (Bandwidth)
2,352 bytes

12 bytes Sync	4 bytes Header	8 bytes Sub-header	2,328 bytes User data

If only disc format compatibility exists, as with the Yellow Book CD-ROM specification, then discs need to be associated with specific computer systems. At a second level it is possible to target at disc format, disc and content identification and at file access compatibility. This was the aim of the High Sierra Group and provided the data content of the disc is text oriented then the means exists to provide a level of compatibility between discs and systems.

However, when dealing with audio and video as well as text, this level of compatibility is insufficient so with CD-I a further level of compatibility is required. This level takes the level described above (the HSG working standard) and adds record access (part of an applications layer) and coding compatibility to provide a total compatibility situation analogous to that existing for CD digital audio discs.

For audio, the CD-I specification defines four levels of sound quality:

1 channel stereo	CD Digital Audio
2 channels stereo or	Hi-Fi Music Mode, 4 channels mono (equivalent to LP music quality)
4 channels stereo or	Mid-Fi Music Mode, 8 channels mono (equivalent to FM broadcast quality)
8 channels stereo or	Speech Mode, 16 channels mono (equivalent to AM broadcast quality)

A channel here is equivalent to 72 minutes' continuous playing time so speech mode represents in excess of 16 hours of speech or a 1 hour speech in 16 languages.

Moving onto video, the CD-I specification distinguishes between resolution requirements and coding. The specified CD-I resolutions are defined as Normal (i.e. the equivalent of current domestic TV receivers) at 384 x 280 pixels and High (i.e. for high-resolution colour monitors and future digital TV receivers) at 768 x 560 pixels. The pictures are generally non-interlaced although interlacing can be used.

Significantly, when comparing CD-I with the Laservision videodisc system, the CD-I specification provides for a World Standard disc, usable on any TV system (PAL, NTSC, or SECAM) with very low distortion effects of about 3.5%.

The picture coding provides for three picture qualities, which are defined as Natural Pictures - equivalent to the best TV studio picture quality and two graphics levels. Natural pictures, using YUV coding, occupy about 325 KB per picture without interlacing. To decrease throughput times and maintain natural picture quality, all Natural Pictures are compressed with DYUV coding to 108 KB.

The First Graphics Mode is based on absolute RGB coding where 15 bit RGB graphics or 8 bit RGB graphics produce crisp pictures at a cost of approximately 215 KB or 108 KB per picture, respectively. The Second Graphics Mode is based on CLUT (colour look up table) graphics. The CLUT mode can, for example, be used as 8 bits out of 24 bits, requiring 108 KB of storage capacity per picture. Compression can reduce this to about 10 KB per picture.

Text can be visualised either by means of a bit map process with data compression or by character encoding via systems or applications software. The bit-map process requires some 5 bytes for each character. The character-encoded texts can either be system text or application text in standardised form using 1 byte per character. Application text can also be encoded on an extended basis with 2 bytes per character. This second byte specifies factors such as colour, font type and character size.

In order to make allowances for poor-quality presentation at the screen edges of a TV set, text is normally limited to 40 characters on 20 lines contained in a safety area of 320 x 210 pixels in the centre of the screen. The high resolution mode allows 80 characters to be presented on up to 40 lines.

The operating system and microprocessor specified for CD-I needed to take into account the requirements of real-time applications such as entertainment. Since real-time applications require executable object code and system calls, a specific microprocessor and operating system are both defined for CD-I. In addition, specifying the microprocessor family and operating system means it is possible to produce discs carrying audio, video, text, binary data and application programmes, which will work on all CD-I drives from all manufacturers. CD-I users can either code text according to the conventions of the operating system, according to the convention defined by the application software or, if text manipulation is not important, by using bit-mapped images of text on discs.

The microprocessor specified for CD-I is the 68000 family (68070). The CD-I Real Time Operating System (CD-RTOS) is based on the real-time operating system OS9 from Microware.

To ensure universal disc/drive compatibility, dedicated hardware and interfaces are required, including specialised chips for video display processing, audio processing and real-time data transfer via the CD-ROM interface. Chips for these purposes will be available to the OEM market.

A CD-I disc will be able to use the CD-I logo provided there is at least one CD-I track on the disc. If CD audio tracks are also present on a CD-I disc then the first CD-I track will contain only essential information such as the Super TOC (Table of Contents) and possibly the bootstrap and file directories. This information, which is typically no more than a few seconds long, is muted if a CD-I disc is played on a CD audio player. If CD audio tracks are present on a CD-I disc they will be located after this first CD-I track. Any other CD-I information is contained in a track after the CD audio tracks.

The Super TOC contains information about the disc size and format as well as identifying the disc alone or as a member of an album by means of various labels. In addition the Super TOC gives information about the disc size and position of the file directory and bootstrap which is required to start-up the CD-I player. The hierarchical file structure which is used allows for opening files in a single seek operation.

As data blocks on a CD-I can be one of three types - video data, audio data or computer data - synchronisation is necessary to ensure that the information which is being read from the disc is directed correctly into the audio, video or computer processors; all the time ensuring that the right pictures and text are viewed at the right moment and in step with each other and accompanying audio.

Before it can be stored on any CD, information must first be prepared or authored in a particular way. For the production of CDs, recording studios are now well equipped to produce the master tapes necessary to make the discs.

For CD-ROM, text and data must be written in computer readable form. Specialist software houses are already active in transferring existing printed or database information into the correct form on magnetic tape, together with the indexes or inverted directories needed for effective searching.

For CD-I, while use can be made of the above services for text and PCM audio, they need to be supplemented further by techniques for ADPCM audio and video processing as well as the integration of the video, audio and computer data. The CD-I specification will lay down the guidelines that need to be followed by specialist software houses in doing this work.

On 2nd April, 1986, just a month after the announcement of CD-I, Philips and Polygram set up a new company called American Interactive Media Inc. (AIM) in order to spearhead the development of software for CD-I in the U.S. According to the press release announcing the formation of the new company, 'AIM's mission is to establish joint venture relationships with companies that will provide software for the CD-I system'. In October 1986, a similar organisation - European Interactive Media Inc. was set up in London to spearhead the development of software for CD-I in Europe.

As a system, CD-I, like CD audio, will be software driven and Philips expect CD-I software to emerge from a variety of market sectors, including the entertainment industry, the computer industry, the publishing industry and the computer games industry. Given the unprecedented nature of the CD-I medium, moreover, much of the software will have to be created from scratch. In theory a publisher could simply transfer a book onto a CD-I disc but the real opportunities presented by CD-I involve interactivity.

Prototype CD-I players will be introduced in the U.S. by late 1987/early 1988 and the first commercial products could be available by mid to late 1988. According to Philips/Sony some 70 companies have already taken a licence for CD-I but it remains to be seen how many decide to pursue it through to the stage of producing commercial products.

Again, the comments of Knowledgeset about the future for CD-I and its possible overlap with some CD-ROM applications are very illuminating. They consider that the announcement of CD-I was premature. CD-I specifies a stand-alone player and although the player can be linked to existing PCs, a CD-I player will be an unlikely peripheral for today's office workstation - the IBM PC and compatibles - for various reasons:

a.   The IBM PC standard is based on the Intel processor family but CD-I specifies the Motorola 68000 microprocessor.

b.   The CD-I display specifications are different from personal computer display standards. Therefore, a CD-I system next to an IBM PC will require a separate display. Few people will accept or can afford two displays on their desk. CD-ROM systems connected to a PC will not require two complete display systems.

c.   The user controls for a CD-I player will also be redundant with the PC keyboard.

In the view of Knowledgeset, CD-ROM drive costs should remain below those for a CD-I player for a number of reasons:

a.   CD-ROM mechanisms will benefit from the manufacturing volume of CD audio and CD-I players;

b.   CD-ROM drives will quickly become half height devices deriving power from the PC's power supply and the controller can be integrated with other controllers on a single board;

c.   CD-ROM drives will contain fewer components than a CD-I player which will include a 68000 CPU, RAM, ROM, user controls, CD-ROM drive and video and audio D/A converters.

The cost and time required to produce CD-I applications that capitalise on the multi-media capabilities will be significant. Many commercial applications do not require a multi-media presentation and cannot afford the disc 'real estate' that they will consume.

In summary, CD-I has clearly been designed for the consumer market and will in all probability have a major impact on the entertainment industry. CD-I can be seen as a multi-media extension of CD audio that includes compressed audio, still frame video, animation and executable code for application specific interactivity. The only caveat that one can enter is that a number of other high technology products that have been aimed at the consumer market - videodiscs and viewdata being just two - have not proved successful and the high costs involved in programming material for CD-I will inevitably slow acceptance of the technology by publishers.

CD-ROM continues to be best suited for commercial applications because it is not CPU or operating system specific and hence should live through several generations of computer hardware. The commercial market is likely to demand that CD-ROMs produced today will remain accessible in the future.

The strength of read only optical data storage is in CD-ROM because, in itself, it has no limits in commercial, educational, entertainment or other markets. The electronic information industry is ready today to build new and profitable markets and businesses. CD-ROM is the base and CD-I is one of many specific standards that will help the growth of this exciting new technology.

We have dealt with CD-I in detail here because it is a new concept and one which needs a lot of explaining in order to demonstrate its relationship to CD-ROM. In addition, as it had not been announced in 1985, CD-I was not covered in Publication 23. The rest of this report is primarily devoted to CD-ROM as, as we have pointed out, no CD-I players or products are currently available but we will refer to CD-I again during the course of the report and in particular in Chapter Five on applications.

1.3   Recordable Digital Optical Disks

As we are looking at optical publishing sytems in this report, our prime focus has been on read only optical media, of which videodiscs, CDs, CD-ROMs and CD-I are the main examples. However, to complete the picture, we felt we must show how closely these read only media relate to recordable and erasable optical disk systems. Recordable disks are, therefore, dealt with here and erasables in the next section.

With recordable DODs, as the name implies, it is possible for the user to record data on the disks himself in-house. Recordable disks are called Write Once Optical Disks (WOODS) or, alternatively, Write Once Read Many (WORM) times disks. Both these terms are slightly misleading as they tend to imply that all the data has to be written at the same time. In fact, users can continue to record data onto sections of the disks over a period of time measured in years until the entire disk is full. In effect, therefore, they are write many times and read many times disks. However, the key point is that any one sector of the disk can only be written on once. It is not possible to overwrite data onto a sector that has already been used or to erase and re-record data on the same sector and so, in that sense, each sector of the disk is write once read many times. This characteristic makes WOODs an ideal archival medium and they are likely to replace magnetic tape in a number of applications as a data archiving medium and, in some applications, microfilm as a way of storing facsimile scanned images of documents.

The processes involved in producing WOODs are very similar, in many respects, to those for read only media but there are also a number of key differences which restrict the potential of recordable disk systems for publishing applications.

a.   The mastering stage - with read only media all the information (video, audio or digital data) is recorded onto the master disc at this stage together with formatting and indexing data and, in some cases, retrieval software. With recordable and erasable/rerecordable media only the formatting and indexing data is recorded at this stage, leaving the rest of the disk blank for users to record their own data onto it at a later stage.

b.   After mastering, the blank formatted disks are replicated in much the same way but instead of simply being coated with a reflective layer and a protective coating - as is the case with videodiscs, CDs, CD-ROMs and CD-Is - the recordable disks are firstly coated with a sensitive recording layer and then a number of different protective treatments are applied and the replicates are usually loaded into plastic cartridges to provide further protection from damage during handling.

c.   At the playback stage, users of recordable optical disk systems require a combined recorder/player rather than simply a player. In the recorder/player (or drive) the optical head comprises either two separate lasers - a high power one for recording and a lower power one for reading - or one laser which can operate at different levels of intensity.

d.   While there is one physical standard for CDs and CD-ROMs and one de facto standard for optical laser videodiscs, there are currently no standards relating to recordable digital optical disks. They are available in a range of diameters including 5.25 inch, 8 inch, 12 inch and 14 inches and they make use of a wide range of substrates (base materials) including glass, aluminium and plastic; a range of different recording mechanisms (pit formimg, bubble forming, phase change, dye ablate); a range of protective measures; single, dual, trilayer or even quadrilayer recording surfaces; grooved or non-grooved tracking and pre-formatted, non-formatted or post-formatted disks.

The result is that, with a few exceptions, each commercially available recordable digital optical disk is designed to play in one particular drive and is not recordable or readable on drives from other suppliers. Hence Optical Storage International (a co-operative venture between Control Data Corporation and Philips) produce a 12 inch recordable digital optical disk (DOD) and a 12 inch single disk drive - the Laserdrive 1200 - and companies who wish to use their disk media must use their drive. Other companies, including Hitachi, have complete proprietary systems.

One exception is Alcatel Thomson Gigadisc, the French company who developed their Gigadisc 12 inch disk and their Gigadisc disk drive. Their media is also playable on the Optimem 1000 disk drive produced by Optimem in the U.S. and media produced by 3M in the U.S.A. and Hoechst in Europe as well as Alcatel Thomson themselves can be played on the ATG Gigadisc drive, so there are a number of second sources of media for the drive.

The above points relate primarily to 12 inch disks, the first WOODS to be launched on the market, and to the first generation of 5.25 inch disks which have been launched by two pioneering companies - Optotech and ISI. Suppliers were so far advanced with commercialisation of incompatible 12 inch WOODs that it was impossible to try and provide for a standard before the disks were launched. There is now some work on physical standards for 12 inch disks but it is at an early stage.

However, with 5.25 inch disks the bulk of the companies developing drives and media (estimated to be in excess of 50 major companies) are delaying production of drives and media because they are awaiting the outcome of the considerable efforts which are currently being made at both national and international level to introduce physical standards for 5.25 inch WOODs (dimensions, clamping, etc.).

The organisations involved include the British Standards Institution, American National Standards Institution and the Japanese Industrial Standards Committee, at the national level and the International Standards Organisation, the European Computer Manufacturers' Association and the International Electro Technical Commission at the international level.

ECMA TC 16 first met in March 1983; ECMA TC 31 first met in February 1984; ANSC X3 BII first met in 1983; BSI OIS/4 first met in February 1985 and ISO/TC 97/SC 23 had its first meeting in May 1985, set up an editing group and was set to hold its second meeting and produce a draft standard in September 1986. TC 31 has held 8 meetings to date and some 82 papers have been published.

There are four main aspects to the 5.25 inch WOOD standard. The first is definitions and environment and this is agreed; the second is mechanical, physical and dimensions and this is almost complete. There was controversy here over whether magnetic or mechanical clamping should be endorsed, but magnetic won the day. The third and fourth sections on optical characteristics and format still need considerable work.

In summary, with 5.25 inch WOODs, considerable progress has been made in the standards field. There is, however, some way to go before an equivalent to the Philips/Sony Yellow Book standard could be agreed for 5.25 inch write once digital optical disks and drives. In the interim the lack of such a standard and the expectation among the industry that such a standard may become available in 1987, is delaying the introduction of such products.

e.   The final difference is in pricing. The read only media are publishing media and hence, while there is a relatively high mastering cost, replicate discs can be produced very cheaply and the players are relatively inexpensive. With recordable DOD systems, there is, of course, no commercial mastering cost as the data is recorded on the disks by users in-house but the disks are relatively expensive at present because the coating process is critical and they have to be supplied with cartridges. Current prices for 12 inch recordable disks range from £200-£500. In addition, the digital optical disk drives are more expensive as they include record capabilities. A typical cost of a 12 inch single disk drive at present is £10,000.

The above will, it is hoped, help make the important point that while read only and recordable optical disks are similar in many respects, there are also significant differences which help to determine the market areas each will serve. CD-ROM is well suited to the distribution of digital databases to a large number of clients but is not suited to the in-house creation and storage of databases as users would have to have a magnetic tape drive on their computer system, send the tape to an intermediary and have them reformat it, produce a master CD-ROM and one or two replicates and then send them back to the user company - an expensive and time consuming exercise which could not be justified unless multiple copies of the database were to be distributed.

In contrast, a recordable digital optical disk would be ideal for archiving in-house databases as the user would simply download data from their computer system onto the recordable disk and it would be stored and instantly available. A number of companies, such as Aquidneck Data Systems, Data General and others offer optical disk data storage subsystems which are designed to emulate magnetic tape drives and link with most host processors and the Central Computing & Telecommunications Agency in the U.K. recently conducted a major experiment to prove the viability of such systems.

However, if the user then wanted to make multiple copies of that database available to other users he would be faced with problems. The only way to copy digital optical disks at present is serially by reading the data from one disk and recording it onto another disk. This is a slow process, akin to copying a videocassette recorder and demands, as a minimum, the availability of two digital optical disk drives. One full disk would take approximately 60 minutes to copy in this way. Even assuming that these problems could be overcome the next problem would be the cost of the disks (£200-£500 each) and the fact that at present they will only play on proprietary drives which, in turn, will only interface with certain computer systems.

In future, if the physical and logical structures of 5.25 inch WOODs are standardised and different disks can therefore be played on different drives then it will be possible to agree an interchange standard, similar to that which exists for magnetic tapes and 5.25 inch WOODs could be used for the exchange of database information. They would not compete with CD-ROMs for distribution to a mass market but could complement them. For example, users of online databases can, in future, expect to be offered the option of purchasing all or a portion of the databases on CD-ROMs for a fixed yearly subscription and they will then be able to search the databases locally on their PCs. Such systems will tend to be single user systems with limited post processing capabilities.

As an alternative, major corporations could also have the option of purchasing, at a higher price, the entire database on a 5.25 inch WOOD and then running it on a host to provide multi-user access to the database and the ability to download major sections of the database - just as today some large corporations will purchase databases on magnetic tape.

One other way in which WOODs will complement CD-ROM systems and be used alongside them is well demonstrated by a system recently introduced by Laserdata and called Laserview. The basic concept is that it enables an in-house or commercial publisher to create his database by keyboarding data and scanning in graphics; to manipulate it and format it on a high resolution screen; to store it on a WOOD and then to output all or subsections of it onto magnetic tape and send the tape for premastering and CD-ROM production. The Laserview system is a small scale system using a 5.25 inch WOOD but major publishers and government departments could make use of customised systems based around 12 inch WOODs stored in jukeboxes, to build up very large databases and then produce many different subsets of the databases for output online or on CD-ROM or other media such as Computer Output Microfiche or paper via a laser printer, depending on the requirements of their marketplace.

Such combined optical publishing systems would bring many advantages and are already being planned and implemented by the major Patent Offices, Government publishing agencies, microform publishers and conventional publishers.

In conclusion, therefore, recordable digital optical disks are for in-house capture, storage and retrieval of coded data and scanned images, they are not primarily a publishing/dissemination medium. They will function primarily as an enabling medium - allowing publishers and in-house users to build up and maintain large mixed mode online databases in-house, comprising both data and raster scanned images, where before the costs of the equivalent amount of magnetic storage would have proved prohibitive.

We must close this brief look at recordable DOD systems with a look at the specifications for some of the first generation systems. The majority of first generation recordable optical disk drives use 12 inch diameter disks, based on the popular videodisc format. The disks offer storage capacities of 1-1.6 Gbytes per side and can be single or double sided.

The OSI Laserdrive 1200 intelligent digital optical disk drive can accept a single sided, 1 Gbyte, 12 inch preformatted glass disk using Philips' air sandwich construction. There are 32,000 tracks per disk with 32 sectors of 1,024 user bytes per track. The drive can be supplied with an ISI or SCSI interface and offers a sustained transfer rate to the host of 250 Kbytes/sec. Average access time is 150 ms and the disk rotates at 480 rpm on the drive. Corrected error rates from the drive are less than 1 in 10^{12} and the drive's Mean Time Between Failure is rated at 12,000 hours. The drive measures 133mm (h) x 483mm (w) x 650mm (d) and weighs 25 kg.

A new generation of 5.25 inch recordable digital optical disks are also now being developed and marketed by companies such as Optotech and ISI. These first generation 5.25 inch disks offer storage capacities of 100-300 Mbytes per side.

The ISI (Information Storage Inc.) 525WC optical disk drive accepts ISI Superstore 2000 optical disk cartridges holding single sided 5.25 inch DODs with a storage capacity of 100 Mbytes formatted and certified. There are 14,900 user tracks on the disk and 32 sectors of 256 user bytes on each track. The drive offers a data transfer rate of 2.5 Mbits/sec and average access times of 200 ms. The disks rotate at 1,800 rpm and the drives provide corrected error rates of 1 in 10^{12}. Mean time between failure for the drive is rated at 15,000 hours. The drive measures 83mm (h) x 146mm (w) x 203mm (d) and weighs 2 kg.

Finally, we may see within two years a recordable CD-ROM which Philips are already referring to as CD-PROM (Compact Disc Programmable Read Only Memory). It would make use of irreversible phase change recording techniques and would offer the same storage capacity, access speeds and data transfer rates as current CD-ROM drives. However, the CD-PROM would be provided in its own cartridge for media protection and would not be readable on a standard CD-ROM drive. Philips will, however, launch a new CD-PROM drive which will be able to play both CD-PROMs and CD-ROMs and potentially CD audio discs. Further details of the CD-PROM development are not available at present but the economics of CD-PROM are likely to resemble those of 5.25 inch write once systems rather than CD-ROM and so, again it is unlikely to have a major impact on optical publishing systems. Specifications for CD-PROM will be contained in, yes you have guessed it, the forthcoming 'Blue Book'.

1.4 Erasable Digital Optical Disks

Erasable DODs can best be viewed as a third generation of optical disks which will give users the ability to not just record data on the disks but the ability to record, erase and re-record data many thousands or even millions of times on the same track sector, just as they can with magnetic media today.

This latter facility is essential for many active computer applications where files need to be retrieved, modified and rewritten on a regular basis and the majority of operations and applications software packages assume the use of erasable media. Hence erasable optical disk suppliers will be aiming to compete directly with both flexible and rigid magnetic disks for a share of the computer storage peripheral market.

The four main advantages that they offer over magnetic media are:

a.   High storage capacity - in excess of 200-300 Mbytes per 5.25 inch disk

b.   Low cost drives.

c.   Removable disks so the off-line storage capacity is unlimited and jukebox type devices could offer automatic disc handling facilities.

d.   Durability as the use of non-contact laser record/read heads could avoid the risk of headcrashes.

As can be seen from Figure 1, the processes involved in mastering and replicating erasable disks are almost identical to those for recordable disks. The mastering stages are the same and much of the replication, but, at the coating stage, the chemical structure of the recording layer is different so that the recording/erasure process can be repeated on a cyclical basis and not be a single, unalterable process.

Although working prototypes of erasable digital optical disk systems have been shown, no erasable systems are commercially available at present and hence exact specifications are hard to give. 3M is one of the leading companies in this area together with KDD, Sharp and other Japanese companies. Two basic techniques are employed - phase change and magneto-optic - and latest estimates are that erasable disk subsystems using these two techniques will begin to become available from 1988 onwards.

Phase change systems are based around the observable fact that certain tellurium based alloys can exist at room temperature in either the crystalline or the amorphous form and can be switched reversibly between each state. The optical properties of the film - its reflectivity - are different for the crystalline and amorphous states and this forms the basis for the optical read-out of the stored data. Matsushita are one of the leading proponents of this recording technique.

The recording of data in magneto-optic systems involves the use of a laser to provide heat and a magnetic coil to provide the magnetic field. Prior to recording, the entire recording layer (the magnetic film) of the disk is perpendicularly magnetised. Then, at the recording stage, a micron sized region on the disk is heated up by the write laser to a point above the so called Curie point and, as the material cools in the presence of an external magnetic field oriented antiparallel to the initial direction of magnetisation, a small region (one micron) is formed that is reverse polarised. This region is the equivalent of a pit or bubble in recordable disks and playback is accomplished with a low power laser read beam using either the M/O Kerr effect or the Faraday effect.

Figure 1

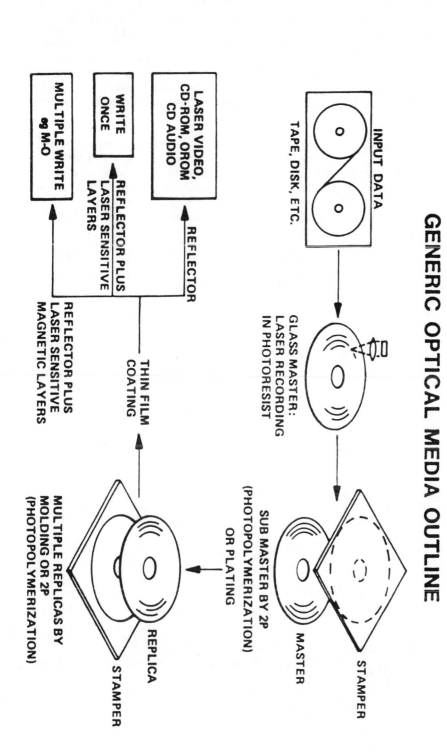

GENERIC OPTICAL MEDIA OUTLINE

The first generation of erasable digital optical disks, when they become widely available, are likely to be 5.25 inches in diameter and will be recorded in CAV mode to provide fast access times and high data transfer rates. 3M have recently formed a co-operative agreement with Optimem in the U.S. to produce and build a universal drive that will accept read only, write once and erasable rewritable 5.25 inch disks recorded in CAV mode. The read only medium used in such a drive would not be CD-ROM but would be a double-sided, 5.25 inch diameter, CAV mode Optical Read Only Memory. This is still a long way off from commercial reality but we discuss the potential of the 5.25 inch Optical Read Only Memory (OROM) and compare it with CD-ROM in Chapter Seven.

Our aim, in this brief run through the range of optical disc systems currently on the market or under development, has been to give the reader a brief survey of the potential of these media and to dispel any misconceptions they may have nurtured about the potential applications for the different disc systems. It will also, hopefully, explain why we and many industry experts consider CD-ROM to be the most promising of the optical storage media for publishing applications in the short to medium term. In the next five chapters of this report we concentrate on CD-ROM and look at all aspects of its use as an optical publishing medium before coming back in Chapters Six and Seven to compare it with the other optical storage media and traditional media such as paper and microfilm.

SUGGESTED READING

HENDLEY, A. M. Videodiscs, compact discs and digital optical disks: an introduction to the technologies and the systems and their potential for information storage, retrieval and dissemination. Cimtech Publication 23, 208 pages. 1985. ISBN 0 85267 245 4. £24.

ROTH, J. Paris (et al). Essential guide to CD-ROM. Meckler Publishing, 190 pages. 1986. ISBN 0 88736 045 9. £29.95

Data Storage on Optical Disk - an experiment. H.M. Treasury, (Central Computer & Telecommunications Agency), London, H.M.S.O. Information Technology in the Civil Service Series No. 13. 26 pages. 1986. ISBN 0 11 330004 2. £6.50

CD-ROM: the new papyrus. Microsoft Press. 620 pages. 1986. ISBN 0 914845 75 6. $39.95

HENDLEY, A. M. The archival storage potential of microfilm, magnetic media and optical data discs. Cimtech Publication 19. 77 pages. 1983. ISBN 0 85267 211 X. £10.

BARRETT, R. Developments in optical disk technology and the implications for information storage and retrieval. BLR&DD Report 5623. Cimtech Publication 18. 80 pages 1981. ISBN 0 905984 714 0. £45

2. STANDARDISATION ISSUES

The attributes of CD-ROM systems, as outlined in Chapter One, should help explain why we are concentrating on CD-ROM based optical publishing systems in this report as we regard them as the most advanced of the optical publishing systems today.

CD-I, when it becomes available, will pose relatively few standards questions as the Philips/Sony Green Book standard defines a complete system which can be adopted and used like the CD audio standard outlined in the Red Book. The only issue is whether or when Philips and Sony will have their de facto standards ratified by ISO.

CD-ROM, however, is a computer peripheral and, as such, must meet the dual requirements of the computing and the publishing industry to ensure its long term success and to attract the sort of investment that will be needed to take it from its present position as a prototype distribution system to a mainstream publishing system. One of the main requirements is for internationally accepted standards governing all aspects of CD-ROMs that could affect system compatibility.

As we have seen in Chapter One, the Philips/Sony Yellow Book standard, based on the CD Red Book, defines the physical dimensions of the disc, the recording techniques, the data format, the main aspects of drive performance, data modulation and the error detection and correction system - in short all the elements needed to ensure physical compatibility between CD-ROM discs and CD-ROM drives. This gives CD-ROM a major advantage over the hybrid videodisc systems referred to above where each supplier developed proprietary data encoding systems, proprietary error detection and correction systems and proprietary hardware - all of which were incompatible.

The next stage relates to the need for a logical format standard - an agreed logical format governing how the data is organised on the CD-ROMs and how the CD-ROMs themselves are identified (the volume, directory and file structures). This is necessary if different operating systems running on different computer hardware are to be able to access the information stored on one CD-ROM. Such a logical volume and file structure standard needs to be built on top of the Yellow Book physical standard.

At this point conventional print and microfilm publishers and many database providers who have not been involved at the programming stage may be wondering what we mean by a logical format. The logical format is, in fact, one of the three key components of a CD-ROM file management system. The file management system stands between the application software running on the computer and the controller which controls the disk drive. A file management system basically comprises software and data structures designed to convert the physical, sector-oriented view of the disc held by its controller into a logical view that the application programme can use. In the case of CD-ROM drives, as described in Chapter One, a CD-ROM drive controller views the CD-ROM disc as a sequence of 2 Kbyte sectors spread over 60 minutes of recording time with 75 sectors in each second of the recording - a total of 270,000 sectors. Viewed logically, however, a CD-ROM disc is a collection of files, each with its own unique name, and the application programme needs to be able to call for a file by name and, once the file is open, read it, however long it is, regardless of the fact that the information in the file has to be read in 2 Kbyte sectors or that each sector has a precise physical address.

A CD-ROM file management system, therefore, is designed to allow users to view the disc as a collection of files. The main factors to be considered in designing a file management system for CD-ROM are covered exhaustively by Bill Zoellick in an article entitled 'Software Development' to which the technical reader is referred (1), all we aim to do here is provide a brief paraphrase to indicate why a logical format standard is needed and to indicate how the design of the logical format can affect the performance of the CD-ROM as a publishing medium.

A complete CD-ROM file management system comprises three major components: the structure or logical format of the data, the software that writes the data in that format (referred to by Zoellick as the origination software) and the software that reads and translates the logical format for our use (which Zoellick refers to as the destination software).

The logical format of the CD-ROM disc will determine where to put identifying data on the disc, where to find the directory or directories of files on the disc, how the directory is structured, whether subdirectories are supported, how many files can be stored on a CD-ROM, the performance cost of storing large numbers of files, how large a file can be, whether files can span multiple volumes and whether files must consist of sequential consecutive sectors.

The logical format must be clearly distinguished from the physical format of the disc, defined in the Philips/Sony Yellow book, which is considered as given by the file management system. Even given this brief outline of the function of the logical format it can hopefully be appreciated how crucial it is to the file management system - it defines the system's structure and operating characteristics and hence must be standardised if CD-ROM compatibility is to be achieved.

The origination software component of a CD-ROM file management system will be dealt with in more detail in Chapter Three when we look at all the stages involved in creating a CD-ROM product. Basically, before mastering a CD-ROM, the files that are going to be recorded on the disc must be assembled and a directory created according to the rules of the logical format. Origination software does that work - effectively providing the writing component of the file system.

The destination software component is the software which runs on the end user's computer which understands the logical format and can use it to provide access to the files on the disc. This destination software is effectively the reading component of the file system.

There is not space in a report of this length to give a detailed account of all the work that has been done in the CD-ROM standardisation area and to trace all the events which led to the publication of a working paper for a standard CD-ROM volume and file structure by a group called the CD-ROM Ad Hoc Advisory Committee. Such an account can be found in a report produced for the Commission of the European Communities on behalf of the European Optical Disc Forum by Julie Schwerin and Tony Hendley (2). Here we give a very brief account of the development of the working standard.

The CD-ROM 'Yellow Book' standard was made available in 1985 and the National Information Standards Organisation (NISO) organised a meeting of information industry representatives to discuss the need for CD-ROM standards. The meeting reached consensus that a minimal standard was needed which allowed interchangeability and supported optimal performance without limiting applications. NISO agreed to develop the standard in their capacity as Committee Z39 of the American National Standards Institute (ANSI) but it took them six months to name a committee, by which time numerous CD-ROM products had been announced.

The committee were charged with developing a standard which should establish a minimum amount to enable:

a.   Developers of software to have a uniform file environment in which to design and implement applications

b.   Publishers and distributors of information to master a single compact disc and know that replicated copies will be readable throughout the world on most combinations of CD players (drives), computer hardware and computer operating systems

c.   Manufacturers of compact disc systems to write a single version of file server software for most computer operating systems

d.   Mastering services to validate replicated copies of compact discs using the directory and other standard information elements to verify accurate placement of data on the disc.

While NISO were naming their committee and drawing up the goals of the standard, Digital Equipment Corporation proposed their own de facto file structure standard for use on read only media and there was a genuine concern that if some working standard for CD-ROM file formats was not agreed quickly, then the number of different CD-ROM products would proliferate and suppliers would become entrenched with their own file structures and there would be no compatibility.

Hence another industry group, referred to as the 'Ad Hoc Committee' or the 'High Sierra Group' (so named from the hotel at which they held their first meeting) met in the autumn of 1985. The High Sierra Group (HSG) included among its members representatives from Apple, Digital Equipment Corporation, Hitachi, Microware/Philips/Sony (the CD-I Group), Microsoft, Reference Technology, 3M, TMS, Videotools, Xebec and Zellick Inc. Together they represented a mix of small innovative companies pioneering the use of CD-ROM publishing systems and major computer hardware and software companies. Their aim was to work together to come up with a working or interim standard for CD-ROM volume and file structures which the industry could use prior to NISO making a ruling. In fact, given the influence of the companies represented on the HSG it was widely believed that, provided a genuine consensus of opinion was reached, their proposal would certainly be adopted as a working standard and would in all probability be accepted as the official standard in due course, with any minor amendments deemed necessary.

In drawing up the functional requirements for the proposed CD-ROM volume and file structure standard, the HSG contacted and received representations from a number of industry associations and committees including the American Library Association's technical standards committee and the U.S. Information Industry Association's standards committee who set up a CD-ROM sub-committee and put forward three main requirements. Since these represented the concerns of the U.S. publishers and information providers they are worth reproducing here in full:

a. A primary functional requirement of a CD-ROM standard is the interchangeability of CD-ROM discs with CD-ROM drives interfaced with various common computers running various common operating systems

b. Since CD-ROM has certain inherent performance limitations in seek times and transfer rates, the CD-ROM standard should support optimised performance of the media/device combination

c. Development of applications for CD-ROM should not in any way be restricted or precluded by the CD-ROM standard. It is understood that the CD-ROM standard cannot ensure the success of the applications, rather it should not restrict their freedom nor inhibit their implementation.

To gain input from as wide a range of interests as possible the HSG put out their own Functional Requirements Questionnaire for the CD-ROM Logical Format and in Europe the technical committee of the Optical Disk Forum met twice in order to provide a response.

The HSG working standard was due to be announced in March/April but the announcement by Philips/Sony of the proposed CD-I standard, caused a delay while the HSG considered the implications of CD-I and made provision for compatibility between the volume and file structures for CD-ROM and CD-I. The HSG held six meetings in all and at their 28th-30th April meeting they reached a consensus. Eventually the 'Working paper for a standard CD-ROM volume and file structure' was released on 28th May, 1986 and copies were sent to NISO and to ECMA (the European Computer Manufacturers Association). Since then the working paper has been reorganised and several substantive changes have been made to it. These were incorporated in a new document - NISO EE-1 Volume and file structure of compact read only optical disks for information interchange - dated 27th August, 1986 and this document, with further minor changes agreed at a recent NISO meeting, is expected to be accepted by ECMA in December 1986 and then ratified by ISO by July 1987.

One other interesting change which occurred was that at the October meeting of the NISO CD-ROM committe in New York, an observer from IBM proposed that the name of the standard be changed from 'Volume and file structure of compact read only optical disks for information interchange' to 'Volume and file structure of read only optical disks for information interchange' in order to make the point that the standard could be applied to other read only optical disk formats, e.g. the proposed OROM CAV format disk (see Chapter Seven). This proposal was accepted by the NISO committee and hence the High Sierra Group standard, when it is finally ratified, will be a standard for read only optical disks of which CD-ROM is currently the only commercially available example. While this move could prove significant in the future, we are primarily concerned here with the effect of the working standard on the acceptability of CD-ROM as a publishing medium and the rest of this chapter is devoted to a further investigation of the benefits that standardisation will bring to the fledgling CD-ROM publishing business.

Again, a detailed consideration of the technical aspects of the standard and its implications for the information industry are beyond the scope of this report and readers are referred to the Optical Disk Forum report on the 28th May version of the standard (2), the main findings of which are not altered by the subsequent changes which have been made to the working paper, and to a subsequent report written by Julie Schwerin with other key members of the High Sierra Group (3). As we have stated, the scope of the standard is at the logical level, it has nothing to do with hardware. It is simply a binary file structure that defines the format that has to be recorded so that when a data preparer wishes to have files put to the CD-ROM that can be read by an applications programme on a PC or minicomputer, everyone will know how to read it.

The HSG proposed standard only specifies the format and not any system requirements. It defines a logical sector which is the greatest of 2,048 bytes or 2^N as that is the largest number that fits in the size of sector on the medium, so given the CD-ROM standard, that means 2,048 bytes in practice. It also defines a logical block size as being a multiple of 512 bytes so applications that wish to force everything to start at sector boundaries can do so. Once the logical sector is defined, there is no reference to hardware in the proposal.

The component specifications are a volume structure, a directory structure and a file structure. The volume structure is such that there are volume descriptors recorded in a fixed location on the medium. Sectors 0-15 on the disc are reserved for operating system use; at logical sector 16 one starts recording volume descriptors and there are five types of volume descriptor specified. The first is the standard file structure volume descriptor which defines the total space recorded on the medium, defines creation dates and logical block size - in short it describes the volume. This is a mandatory descriptor and all the identifiers are interpreted as using the ISO 646 character set - which implies the use of the English language. To meet the requirements of the European, Japanese and worldwide information industry, the HSG added another type of volume descriptor, referred to as a coded character set file structure volume descriptor, that allows one to use non-English language names for the volume and file name and publisher identifier and one can use as many of these as one wants - catering for multilingual publications on CD-ROM. This is the first volume file structure standard that has done this.

In addition to the above two volume descriptors pointing to essentially directory structures, provision is made for creating one or more volume partitions and pointing to them via volume descriptors referred to as unspecified structure volume descriptors. Such partitions could prove to be another standard file structure or they could be an MS DOS file system.

The fourth is a boot record version which allows a user to identify a system and boot it from the disc and the fifth type is a volume descriptor sequence terminator which simply names the disc and the level of the standard which is being used and terminates the sequence.

The working standard also defined multi-volume volume sets. A volume is defined as a dismountable CD-ROM and a volume set is a collection of one or more volumes on which a volume set is recorded. There are many applications that will require multi-volume files (files that occupy more than one CD-ROM) and multi-volume volume sets and the working standard makes provision for up to 32K volumes in a volume set.

The HSG have also provided a mechanism for adding a volume to an existing volume set without requiring the data preparer to remaster the existing volumes. A volume set shall be the set of volumes on which a file set is recorded. All volumes in a volume set shall be numbered consecutively starting from 1. All volumes in a volume set shall contain a description of the directory hierarchy and the files in each directory for those volumes of the volume set which have the same or lower number as that of the volume containing the description. Such a description, recorded on a volume, shall supersede the description recorded on any lower numbered volume of the volume set not containing the same value in the volume set size field. Hence, if a user knows he will be adding a volume to the volume set, he has to mount the last volume to the volume set to find out whether he has done it. If he does not mount the last volume to the volume set then it is treated as if the last volume never existed.

The working standard proposes the use of path tables which essentially describe the directory structure recorded on the volume set. The proposed standard provides a path table for fast access to each directory and a logically hierarchical directory structure with a maximum of 8 levels. The entire directory structure can be in one place on the disc or it can be split up and parts of the directory recorded throughout the CD-ROM, near the data. Each directory can hold an unlimited number of files and there is no limit to the size of the files. In addition the working standard makes provision for multi-extent files and for interleaving files.

The working standard provides for both unstructured bit-stream information in files - no record structures, the application-dependent interpretation of the data in the file - and also specifies a hook to a record structure so that the CD-ROMs can be used, if required, with standard performing programming languages.

Finally, the standard specifies three nested levels of interchange:

> Level 1 is restricted so MS-DOS can read it - there is the stipulation that a file name shall not contain more than 8 d-characters and a file name extension shall not contain more than 3 d-characters.

> Level 2 is set up to be a proper subset of what the HSG believe the CD-I people are going to do.

> Level 3 has everything.

Since it has been released the HSG working standard has been studied and commented on by a number of industry groups to see whether it meets the functional requirements put forward and, specifically, whether it meets the goals set by NISO and IIA which were listed above.

Taking the NISO goals first, provided it is adopted, the HSG working paper would certainly enable developers of software to have a uniform file environment in which to design and implement applications.

Again, provided it is adopted, the HSG working paper should enable manufacturers of CD-ROM drives to write a single version of file server software for most computer operating systems.

The HSG working paper would also enable mastering services to validate replicated copies of compact discs using the directory and other standard information elements to verify accurate placement of data on the disc.

The fourth goal of NISO was that the standard should enable publishers and distributors of information to master a single compact disc and know that replicated copies will be readable throughout the world on most combinations of CD players (drives), computer hardware and computer operating systems.

As described in Chapter One, the High Sierra Group working paper, on its own, will not entirely fulfil this goal and it is doubtful whether it will ever be fully realised in the publishing environment but the working paper certainly represents a major step forward towards it. For this goal to be fully achievable one would also need standard hardware and software interface supports from the operating systems to the range of CD-ROM drives on the market and a standard hardware interface from the CD-ROM drives to the computer systems. In addition, publishers would have to use standard indexing and retrieval software packages that could run on all the main operating systems on all the main computer hardware. Such software, if it were ever developed, would undoubtedly suffer from severe limitations but it could perhaps be used in certain applications where publishers simply distributed a set of files on CD-ROM and PC users simply ran a utility piece of software to search the directory and download specific files from the CD-ROM onto their magnetic disk for subsequent processing.

Looking at the database publishing application, however, where free text retrieval will be required, it appears certain that, for the short to medium term at least, publishers will have to form close arrangements with the suppliers of retrieval software and there will be a fixed relationship between the structuring of at least the index file if not the full text file on the CD-ROM and the retrieval software that has been selected for use. Inevitably, therefore, if a publisher chooses to use a software package that only runs on one operating system he will limit the potential market for his CD-ROM database.

Moving on to consider the three functional requirements specified by the IIA sub-committee, the first requirement - the interchangeability of CD-ROM discs with CD-ROM drives interfaced with various common computers running various common operating systems - simply reiterates the fourth goal of NISO listed above and the same points apply (the HSG working paper takes us some way towards that goal but certainly not all the way).

The second requirement was that, since CD-ROM has certain inherent performance limitations in seek times and transfer rates, the CD-ROM standard should support optimised performance of the media/device combination.

This relates to a number of points which were made in Chapter One concerning the physical characteristics of CD-ROM derived from its base in CD audio format.

As we have said before, CD-ROM is a read only medium. This can be seen as a limitation when looking at CD-ROM as a computer peripheral but when viewed as a publishing medium, CD-ROM's read only nature is a positive advantage.

Many in the computer industry tend to look at CD-ROM as a temporary phenomenon - the first of a new generation of optical storage media which will culminate in erasable digital optical disks. The logical result of this view would be that any directory and file structure for CD-ROM would need to be designed to be extendable to erasable media and would, therefore, not primarily be designed to optimise the performance of CD-ROM as a read only publishing medium.

For publishers and information providers, however, CD-ROM is not the stepping stone to future media products, it is a read only medium that can be used in the near future by the millions of PC and minicomputer users worldwide and they want a file structure designed specifically for a read only medium that will allow database preparers and software suppliers to optimise the performance of CD-ROM as a publishing and data distribution medium. The IIA and the Optical Disk Forum in Europe have taken this latter approach, insisting that the working standard be designed to optimise the performance of read only media and not to be easily extendable to erasable media and this approach is embodied in the IIA's second functional requirement.

What specifically do we mean by optimising CD-ROM's performance as a read only publishing medium? As we have seen in Chapter One, CD-ROM offers very high storage capacity - 550 Mbytes (formatted) - but relatively slow access or seek times of from 0.5 to 1 seconds due to the use of CLV mode recording where the rotational speed of the disc has to be changed and the data cannot be addressed as quickly or as accurately as with CAV mode. Compared to standard fixed magnetic disk drives CD-ROM seek times are five to ten times slower and compared to high performance magnetic disk drives CD-ROM seek times are some twentyfive to fifty times slower. Hence the need for a CD-ROM file management system which optimises the performance of CD-ROM based publications by minimising the number of seeks that have to be made to open files and conduct complex searches.

However, while the slow access times offered by CD-ROMs do pose problems, there are other attributes of CD-ROM which can offer significant benefits to system integrators. Due to the fact that the laser read head can be focused onto any one of a number of adjacent tracks without moving the read arm, rapid seeks can in fact be made to adjacent tracks on a CD-ROM and once the data is accessed, it can be read off the discs at an acceptable rate of approximately 1.4 Mbits/sec - two facts which offer scope for innovative system designers to improve the performance of CD-ROM products by grouping related data together in large blocks prior to recording it on the disc.

Perhaps the greatest benefit of all, however, derives from CD-ROM's read only nature.

Firstly, CD-ROM is a read only publishing medium so data is written to a master once and then replicates are made and sent out to users to read via a drive and their own computer. The users cannot write to the CD-ROM or change any of the files so when designing directories and directory structures for CD-ROM, there is no need to cater for deletions, insertions, overflows, modifications and many of the other problems which have to be catered for when designing the directories for erasable media. Hence with CD-ROM there is scope for simplifying the design and structure of directories and for organising them in such a way as to facilitate searching for files and hence improving the performance.

Secondly, and a related point, because CD-ROM publications are written once by the publisher/system integrator, and then are going to be read many times by a number of users, there is an opportunity and, indeed, a requirement to put considerable effort into the organisation, indexing and formatting of the database in order to make it easy to access and search by the end user. We shall describe the processes involved in producing a CD-ROM product in more detail in Chapter Three but one significant point is that the data creation and manipulation will be done, in the majority of cases, on a powerful minicomputer or mainframe whereas the majority of users will be searching the database using a lower power PC so clearly all the necessary formatting and inversion will be done in batch mode at the creation stage.

At the risk of oversimplification, the point which needs to be made here is that given the physical characteristics of CD-ROM, the read only nature of the medium, the economics of publishing and the fact that the database is going to be created once on a powerful computer system and read back many times by a large number of users on lower power PCs, considerable ingenuity, time and effort needs to be spent in planning, organising and indexing a CD-ROM database and any CD-ROM logical format standard must support the efforts of the publishers/data preparers and system integrators to produce effective CD-ROM publishing systems that optimise the potential of CD-ROM as a read only publishing medium.

This point has clearly been taken into consideration by the High Sierra Group in preparing the Working Paper. Prior to the issue of the working paper a number of members of the High Sierra Group had published papers outlining various approaches to the problem of reducing the number of seeks required to open files on CD-ROMs containing large numbers of files. File tables and hashing techniques were suggested and discussed by a number of companies. The Working Paper actually specifies the use of a path table for providing fast access to each directory and a logical hierarchical directory structure with a maximum of 8 levels as that is all some operating systems will support. According to the working paper, the entire directory structure can be in one place on the disc or it can be split up and parts of the directory recorded throughout the CD-ROM, near the data.

The path table will be read into the computer memory once to eliminate future seeks there and, in addition, if the directory is broken up into small directories placed adjacent to the relevant files and data, then those directories can also be read into memory as required and all the files within that directory accessed without any additional seeks.

Hence there is scope, using the working standard, to provide well designed systems which minimise the number of seeks required to gain access to large numbers of files. According to a member of the HSG if the system designer allocates 20 Kb of buffer memory to the path table then up to 40,000 files could be accessed in this way.

The technical committee of the Optical Disk Forum have analysed the main provisions of the standard and their view is that it certainly meets the needs of those who are looking at CD-ROM as a publishing medium and seeking to optimise its performance in that application and hence it can be seen to meet the second requirement made by the IIA.

The third requirement of the IIA was that 'development of applications for CD-ROM should not in any way be restricted or precluded by the CD-ROM standard. It is understood that the CD-ROM standard cannot ensure the success of the applications, rather it should not restrict their freedom nor inhibit their implementation'. This is the same principle of minimality that was enunciated by NISO and it is commonly agreed by industry experts that the standard meets this requirement too.

The full 'Working Paper for a standard CD-ROM volume and file structure' was discussed at a meeting of the European Optical Disk Forum in Luxembourg and delegates to the meeting, representing the European information industry, were asked to complete a questionnaire which sought their response to the standard, whether they would adopt it and whether they felt it would advance the market for CD-ROM publishing products. The full results of the questionnaire are presented in the Schwerin/Hendley report on the standard issued by the Optical Disk Forum (2) and generally the results were very positive with no-one saying they would not adopt the standard and most planning to adopt it within six months. Most also felt it would be a significant factor in opening up the market for CD-ROM publications but by no means the only factor, other issues (including the hardware/software interface question described above and economic and marketing issues) still remain to be resolved before the CD-ROM market reaches its full potential.

In summary, therefore, considerable efforts have been made to standardise CD-ROM systems. The Philips/Sony Yellow book is a de facto standard governing the physical aspects of CD-ROM and the High Sierra Group working paper, which assumes the existence of the Yellow Book standard, standardises the logical format. It remains for these de facto standards to be adopted by ANSI and ISO but it is expected that they will be in due course and in the meantime the industry has working standards to build on.

The logical format standard will certainly facilitate the interchange of data on CD-ROMs but it will not, on its own, meet all the requirements of the publishing industry, some of which may not ultimately prove attainable.

The next desirable development would be to see industry standard hardware and software interface supports from the operating systems to the range of CD-ROM drives on the market and a standard hardware interface from the CD-ROM drives to the computer systems. Until that happens retrieval software vendors and CD-ROM data preparation companies will still have to develop and supply separate software drivers for each combination of CD-ROM drive and operating system.

REFERENCES

1. ZOELLICK, B. CD-ROM software development. Byte Magazine, May 1986 pp 177-188.

2. SCHWERIN, J and HENDLEY, A. M. International initiatives for CD-ROM standards. Unpublished. Available from Learned Information Ltd., Woodside, Hinksey Hall, Oxford OX1 5AU.

3. SCHWERIN, J. (et al). CD-ROM standards: the book. Learned Information Ltd., Woodside, Hinksey Hall, Oxford OX1 5AU. £50. ISBN 09049 33547.

3.   STAGES IN THE PRODUCTION OF CD-ROM DATABASES/PUBLICATIONS

In this chapter we aim to outline all the main stages which have to be gone through before a publisher/information provider can provide copies of a database on replicate CD-ROM discs and to describe the infrastructure that is beginning to grow up and will need to be very firmly established in order to support publishers in the production of such CD-ROM databases on a regular scheduled timetable.

The type and volume of data that is being and will be placed on CD-ROM varies dramatically. The way in which that data is organised will also vary widely depending on the application. It is not surprising, therefore, that the software vendors and data preparation companies who specialise in preparing the data prior to recording it on CD-ROM are developing a range of different services based around software that runs on a wide range of hardware, to cater for all requirements. Rather than attempt to describe all the ever changing range of services offered by the growing number of companies providing software and data preparation services, we decided to limit ourselves here to providing a conceptual account of the stages involved in producing a CD-ROM product and only refer to specific suppliers to illustrate points or provide examples of a particular approach. In Chapter Five we look at some of the main application areas where CD-ROMs are or will be used. In Chapter Eight we list the main companies providing CD-ROM hardware, services and systems and the reader is recommended to contact them directly for further details of their services.

It is inevitable that certain data preparers will call the various production stages we have identified here by different names and perhaps even streamline the process by merging one stage into another but our aim is to provide information providers with a simplified account of the processes involved in producing a CD-ROM database so that they can make a realistic assessment of the costs and resources that will be involved, the services that they will need to call upon and the likely timetable for CD-ROM production and compare the processes involved in producing a CD-ROM publication with the processes involved in producing paper, microfilm and other electronic publications.

In the first two chapters we have established that CD-ROM systems need to be viewed at at least three different levels.

The first level - the physical level as laid down in the Yellow Book - defines the physical characteristics of the disc and the data format and provides for a basic level of compatibility at the physical level (all CD-ROMs can physically be read by all CD-ROM drives).

The second level is the organisational, or logical, level where the High Sierra Group working paper lays down a logical format standard which provides for data to be organised on CD-ROM in a form which, given the necessary hardware and software interfaces between drives, computers and operating systems, will enable it to be accessed by multiple operating systems running on a range of computer hardware. Currently a number of proprietary file formats are employed but over the next year we would expect more and more publishers and data preparers to adopt the High Sierra Group working standard.

The third level is the publishing or database level where the publisher co-operates with a vendor of retrieval software, organises and indexes his database to their specifications and makes available the retrieval element of the software package to users to access the database on CD-ROM as efficiently as possible via a PC.

Physically, the data has to be formatted in 2,048 byte sectors of user data with the required synchronisation, header and auxiliary data fields and the agreed error detection and correction systems. Logically, the data has to be organised according to a logical format standard (a proprietary standard or, increasingly, the High Sierra Group working standard with the path tables; directory hierarchy and volume descriptors specified in that format) and, at the publishing level, the database has to be organised, indexed and inverted according to the requirements of particular software vendors.

Bearing in mind the above three sets of requirements, we must now look in detail at each of the stages involved in producing a CD-ROM database.

3.1   Choice of database

The first stage, of course, is to identify an existing database or collection of data which is well suited to distribution on CD-ROM or to step back and plan a new database or publication that takes full advantage of the strengths and weaknesses of CD-ROM as a distribution medium. Chapters Five to Eight all deal with the choice of databases from different angles, looking at the main application areas where CD-ROM systems will be used, comparing CD-ROM systems with existing paper, online and microfilm distribution systems and looking at some of the early CD-ROM products. All we will attempt to do here is indicate some of the factors involved in choosing material to distribute on CD-ROM.

Firstly, when comparing CD-ROM with paper or microfilm systems, we would suggest that the database has to be active and one whose value is increased by allowing users to access and search it in many different ways. With paper and microfilm, data has to be listed according to one or a limited number of criteria, e.g. by author, title, part number or customer number . If users wish to access the database by one of ten or more different parameters or by searching the full text of the database then this can only be accommodated by making the database available online or on CD-ROM.

Secondly, when comparing CD-ROM to an online system, one of the main considerations has to be the currency of the data. Given that CD-ROM is a publishing medium and the database has to be prepared, premastering has to be done, the CD-ROM master has to be created, replicates stamped out and sent to users, there is inevitably going to be a minimum turnaround time or update cycle. The exact turnaround time will depend on many factors such as the size and complexity of the database and the number of replicates required but currently a month is realistic. Hence CD-ROM will not compete with online databases for making available volatile information such as stock prices and exchange rates. CD-ROM will tend to be used for relatively static databases to which data is added at regular intervals or for data which changes at fixed periods (e.g. timetables which change on a monthly basis or directories which are produced quarterly).

Thirdly, while CD-ROMs could be used to distribute databases as small as 5-10 Mbytes in some applications, the economics of CD-ROM publishing are most attractive when large databases of 100-300 Mbytes are being distributed. In these applications CD-ROM would certainly score over microfilm and paper based systems on consumable costs.

Fourthly, as CD-ROM is a publishing medium and there is a high data preparation and mastering cost (as outlined later in this chapter) followed by low disc replication costs, publishers need to identify either a potentially large number of end users willing to purchase the CD-ROM publication or a fairly small number of users willing to pay a high price for the CD-ROM publication. CD-ROM publishing runs could be cost effective at 100 plus but will prove most attractive in quantities over 1,000.

Clearly there are many other factors involved and these will be addressed in future chapters when considering specific application areas or comparing CD-ROM with other media.

3.2   Data Capture

Having identified the data, the next stage involves capturing it and placing it in a form which can be accepted by either the software vendor who is going to organise and index the database for the publisher or the data preparation house which is simply going to format and premaster the data prior to placing it on CD-ROM.

For the purposes of this report we are going to simplify the situation and look at three scenarios which could face any information provider or publisher considering the use of CD-ROM.

The first is that the material which he wishes to place onto CD-ROM is textual data which already exists in coded ASCII or EBCDIC form. This is the simplest situation and would enable the information provider to go straight on to the next stage which is to plan the organisation of the database in conjunction with a software vendor.

The second is that the data comprises textual information - typewritten or handwritten - which is not in machine-readable form. In this case the information provider would have to arrange for all the text to be keyboarded or OCR scanned. These are both time consuming and expensive procedures and would add considerably to the overheads of any CD-ROM publishing project. However, they would represent a one-off cost and if the information provider is planning a long-term publishing project then the cost of such a conversion exercise can be borne. In addition, of course, the data, once captured, could be used in online, paper or microfilm distribution systems as well as in CD-ROM systems. Once the data is converted into machine readable form then the information provider can again go on to plan the organisation of the database.

The third is that the database comprises photographic or other graphic material which cannot be keyboarded or that the store of textual information on paper or microfilm is potentially so large that keyboarding or OCR scanning is not an economic proposition and all that can be done is to capture facsimile images of each page, as with a microfilm system. In this case the pages containing the graphics or text will be raster scanned using CCD array scanners which convert a page image into a series of picture elements or pixels, each of which can be digitally coded to represent black or white information or shades of gray.

Such scanning systems are used in facsimile machines and there are resolution standards laid down by an international body called the CCITT. However, such scanning systems suffer from three main disadvantages when compared to keyboarding or OCR capture. Firstly, an A4 page scanned at 200 ppi using a simple black-and-white threshold, requires close to 4 Mbits of data to represent it and even after standard data compression algorithms have been applied the storage requirement is still 30-40 times higher than for standard coded text. It has been calculated that approximately 200,000 pages of coded text can be stored on one CD-ROM compared with only about 6,000 scanned images.

The second disadvantage, of course, is that the text contained on the scanned pages cannot be searched and hence each image has to be manually indexed and pages can only be retrieved via keyword searching.

Finally, if high resolution scanned images are stored on a CD-ROM then special high resolution terminals will be required to view the images once they have been retrieved and high quality laser printers will be needed to provide hardcopy. This will add considerably to the price of CD-ROM workstations. We look at the problem of handling images on CD-ROM in more detail in Chapter Four on workstations and Chapter Seven where we compare CD-ROM with microfilm.

Coded graphics, including CAD graphics and chemical symbols can also cause problems for CD-ROM database publishers and are an area where further standards work needs to be done.

3.3   Database creation

Once the relevant data has been captured, the next stage is to begin to organise the database so that the data is easily accessible and meets the search requirements of potential users.

In theory, if a computer supplier or the supplier of a particular system - a CAD system or a desktop publishing system - wanted to simply use CD-ROM as a data interchange medium it would be possible, using the High Sierra Group's logical format or their own proprietary file format, to simply record a set of files on the CD-ROM which could be accessed via a utility piece of software, designed to run on a particular operating system, which would access the directory on the CD-ROM and then access the files. If this is all that is required then the information supplier could go straight on to the data preparation stage described in section 3.4 below.

However, the majority of information providers who are considering using CD-ROM to distribute information will want to make the most of the facilities offered by CD-ROM and maximise the value of their information by organising it as a database - a set of records in an accessible sequence organised so that the data can be read by a retrieval programme - and offering free text retrieval facilities to their potential users.

Fast free text retrieval facilities have been available to users of online databases held on mainframes for many years with companies such as BRS, Harwell and Battelle specialising in the supply of such free text search software packages. Recently, too, with the growth in importance of the mini and microcomputer market, a number of these companies have modified their existing packages and developed new free text retrieval packages for use on smaller computers. An excellent introduction to text retrieval and the range of such text retrieval packages on the market has been produced by the IIS (1).

When it comes to making large databases available on CD-ROM and searchable via text retrieval software that runs on PCs it is not surprising, therefore, that Battelle, BRS and other suppliers of microcomputer based free text retrieval software should be offering to design and index prototype and, in some cases, commercial CD-ROM databases for publishers.

Clearly, if they wish to offer such free text retrieval facilities with their CD-ROM databases, the publishers will have to co-operate closely with one of these software suppliers and plan, organise, index and invert their CD-ROM database to that vendor's specifications.

Many of the processes involved in planning, organising, indexing and inverting a database for CD-ROM publication today will simply follow the processes established for creating an online database and they are already well documented so we will not attempt to describe them in detail here. What we wish to stress is simply the different stages involved in the production of a CD-ROM database and the ways in which they inter-relate. The first stage is to capture the data; the second stage is to design, convert and load the database; the third stage is to define the directory structure and other elements of the logical format (following the High Sierra Group working standard if desired) and to map the database and directory onto magnetic tape in 2,048 byte blocks; the fourth stage is pre-mastering and the fifth stage is to master and replicate the CD-ROM disc.

The following is a very broad outline of the steps involved in designing, converting and loading a database.

a.   The first stage, as outlined above in the section on data capture, is to ensure that the data exists in ASCII coded form on magnetic tape.

b.   The second stage is for the information provider and the software vendor to consult together and plan the database. Specifically, this involves analysing the content of the database, designing the structure of the database so that related data is kept close together and the organisation of the database facilitates its usage, analysing the likely usage of the database, profiling the end users and their method of working and level of computer expertise. The user profile will help the software vendor devise the most appropriate interface - whether menu based or command based - and the ideal screen format.

Space only permits us to list each of these issues but it should be stressed that each issue - screen format, user interface, etc. could be the subject of a separate report and each is crucial to the long term success of CD-ROM publishing. If CD-ROM publications are to be widely used by non-computer and information science professionals in the future then the user interfaces will have to be far more friendly than those currently available with online systems.

c.   The next stage is to divide the database or data file up into a series of logical constructs which are variously referred to as records or documents. Depending on the type of database these could be literally bibliographic records or records relating to a person or they could be articles or sections in a large text file. These records in turn will need to be divided up into fields - the size and shape of which will also be designed to meet the requirements of the application - which allow the user to narrow the range of his search. The records then need to be structured to meet the requirements of the application, screen formats designed, decisions made on whether fixed or variable length fields or both are required and a set of descriptors or headers defined for each record which will be retrieved and used to identify the records retrieved as the result of a search.

d.   The next stage is to define whether all or just a part of each record is to be searchable - the rest of the information in the record can be designated as retrievable, viewable and printable but not searchable. In addition to this, even within the area of the record which is searchable, it is necessary to define a stop word list - a list of common words such as and; but; not etc which are of no value when conducting a full text search.

e.   The final stage we are leaving as a miscellaneous section to cover application specific requirements such as the handling of non standard character sets, chemical formulae, computer graphics and digitised images.

Once these planning stages have been gone through, the database will need to be formatted prior to being loaded. Formatting can be carried out by the software vendor or it can be done in-house by the information provider who simply follows the requirements laid down by the vendor for data submission.

The formatted data is inverted using a specific software programme running on a high power computer - the DEC VAX range are used by most software vendors. Each record in the database is processed and every significant word in each searchable field is extracted and stored, along with a corresponding record number, field identifier and a location identifier for that word, in order to build up an occurrence list or inverted file.

Once the inversion is complete and the desired user interface/screen format has been designed as a result of stage two above, then the next stage is to create the directory structure and map out the database onto the master magnetic tape from which the master CD-ROM will be produced. This is the data preparation stage which is described below.

3.4 Data preparation

With the data captured and the database designed, as described above, the next stages are to build the directory that will be used to locate the data on the CD-ROM disc and to build physically the image of the CD-ROM database on magnetic tape.

As we pointed out above, up to this point the stages outlined would have to be gone through whatever medium the database was destined to be recorded on. At the data preparation stage, however, the process has to be geared specifically to the requirements of CD-ROM.

If the database files were being loaded onto a standard random access erasable magnetic disk then a reserved segment of the disk containing the volume directory would be updated to indicate their arrival, their location and other information. In addition to the volume label or name the volume directory would contain information about every file on the disc including the file name, the start address, the file length and, if required, information about creation date, file organisation and access privilege. The construction of the volume directory and the maintenance of its entries is the responsibility of the computer system's operating system.

In the case of CD-ROM, however, while it is, of course, necessary to construct a similar directory and insert the various statistics which describe the files to be loaded on the disc, this is not the responsibility of any particular operating system. Rather, it is the responsibility of the disc producer or data preparation facility to define the volume directory and to ensure that correct entries are inserted.

To create the volume directory and the file structure the disc producer must write a file structure creation programme and currently there are a number of proprietary programmes designed to create a number of proprietary file structures. Any volume directory structure can be defined but, of course, it is then the responsibility of the disc producer to produce CD-ROM device drivers to interpret the directory correctly so that the required data can be transferred to the search programme. Constructing such a directory involves reading back each file to determine its length.

Now that the High Sierra Group have outlined a working file format standard which seems likely to be adopted by most disc producers in time, it will be possible for the disc producers to each devise one file structure creation programme that complies with the format specified by the High Sierra Group and, more significantly, it should pave the way for the CD-ROM drive manufacturers and the operating system suppliers to co-operate and provide the necessary device drivers and file servers so the disc producers no longer need to produce their own device drivers and file servers but rather can assume their existence. It must be stressed, however, that at present this is not the case. The High Sierra Group working paper is the first step in that direction only.

Once the directory has been constructed the final stage in this process is for the various files that constitute the database to be concatenated together and, together with the directory, to be re-blocked into 2 Kbyte blocks of data. (This matches the physical characteristics of CD-ROMs, as described in Chapter One. Data is recorded onto a CD-ROM in a single spiral track which is divided up into minutes, seconds and seventy-fifths of a second (sectors). Each sector holds 2,352 bytes of data of which 2,048 bytes is user data and represents the smallest addressable data segment on the disc.) The output from this process will then be recorded onto high quality 1,600 bpi magnetic tape ready for pre-mastering.

3.5 Pre-mastering

The next step in the process is technically referred to as pre-mastering. This can be done either by a data preparation facility or by the CD-ROM mastering facility themselves. Basically, pre-mastering comprises taking the database in 2 Kbyte blocks and adding the 12 bytes of synchronisation data, 4 bytes of header data and the 288 bytes of additional error detection and correction coding that are specified in the Yellow Book standard. This pre-mastering process is fully covered by the standard and the result of the process is a 3/4 inch VCR tape which essentially contains the original data in a high quality audio format.

As mentioned above, as with any new industry in the early stages of development, the terminology is not yet accurately defined. Many people will use pre-mastering to refer to the entire data preparation process, others will use the term data preparation to describe the entire database creation, directory definition and pre-mastering processes.

3.6 Mastering and Replication

The next step is the actual creation of the CD-ROM master disc. At this stage, as described in Chapter One and in Cimtech Publication 23 in more detail (2), the CD-ROM is treated just like an audio disc. The tape supplied as the result of the pre-mastering process described above is decoded and the disc is cut. Some mastering facilities offer a check disc facility at this stage which is extremely useful, particularly if the database is complex and has been created for the first time or if a large number of replicate discs are to be produced eventually.

With the check disc option, rather than cutting an expensive master disc initially, a more easily produced glass disc is offered for the publisher or data preparation facility to check their CD-ROM before making a final commitment to producing the master and the required number of replicates. This check disc has a limited life and cannot be used to replicate discs but it does provide a useful opportunity to test the performance of the final CD-ROM product. If the check disc is satisfactory, it will then be necessary to cut the master disc from which stampers can be produced.

As with the normal replication of gramophone records or CDs, replication involves stamping copies from a number of sub-masters or stampers. The labels are added to the replicate discs and the final result is replicate CD-ROMs loaded into the familiar CD cases which can then either be shipped to the publisher or the data preparation facility or direct to the customer.

3.7 What services are available?

Whether an information provider needs to use a commercial company to provide help with all the above five stages or just a few will depend on such factors as their size, their computing resources, their level of commitment to CD-ROM publishing and the size and complexity of the database.

A number of companies can currently offer publishers and information providers a complete service from data capture at one end to the distribution of replicate discs to customers at the other end and even the supply or lease of retrieval hardware. In the U.K., companies offering such a service include Digital Equipment Corporation, Pergamon Infoline, BRS (Europe) and a number of smaller start-up companies including Silver Platter, Archetype and Office Workstations Ltd.

Clearly such companies do not themselves carry out all the work involved in all the stages mentioned above. All of them would use external mastering and replication facilities. In addition, Archetype are agents for TMS, a data preparer in the U.S., and IME; Office Workstations Ltd. are agents for Computer Access Corporation in the U.S.; Pergamon Infoline use Knowledgset's retrieval software and PDSC's data preparation hardware and software and DEC use Battelle's MicroBASIS full text retrieval software. Nevertheless all the above companies would take responsibility for ensuring that all the stages were carried out satisfactorily, leaving the publisher/information provider to plan the subject content and the marketing of the product.

Such a 'one-stop' service is attractive at this stage in the development of CD-ROM, for a number of reasons:

a.   Most publishers and information providers are simply at the stage where they want to experiment with the technology - produce prototype systems to get a fuller picture of the costs involved, the timetables involved, the technical issues and the performance factors. For them a contract with one company to help them through all the stages of CD-ROM production is almost certainly the most cost-effective way to achieve those aims.

b.   The file format working standard has not yet been officially adopted and it will take another 6 months to 1 year before it is widely adopted by data preparers and the necessary file structure creation programmes are developed. It will also take time before standard interfaces are provided between operating systems and CD-ROM drives. Until these building blocks are in place the best way to get a CD-ROM product out to customers for evaluation and use is to design a complete package that is software and hardware specific and one way to achieve that goal is to deal with one company.

c.   If publishers want to carry out the database creation, data preparation and pre-mastering stages in-house then they will need to invest in relatively expensive hardware and pay substantial licensing fees for the rights to inversion software programmes. They will not want to commit themselves at this level until they have definite plans to produce commercial CD-ROM publications and before they can draw up those plans they will need to have produced several test discs.

d.   No one publisher, at this stage at least, is going to invest the 30-50 million pounds required to set up CD-ROM mastering and replication facilities. For the foreseeable future they will have to deal with the commercial mastering and replication facilities and again, the companies offering complete CD-ROM services are well placed to act as intermediaries between the publishers and the mastering facility, ensuring that timetables are met, that standards are adhered to and that discs are checked for quality.

In the short to medium term, therefore, we see a major role for the intermediary companies. In future, when databases have been designed and it is simply a matter of updating and reissuing them, publishers and information providers could cerainly conduct the database inversion and indexing, data preparation and pre-mastering in-house - simply paying a license to the software vendor and calling him in to amend and maintain the software.

For publishers to set up mastering and replication facilities inhouse we would have to see some dramatic breakthroughs in the design of CD-ROM mastering and replication processes and plant.

At the retrieval end, if the file standard is adopted and standard interfaces become available from operating systems to CD-ROM drives, then there will be less need for publishers or even system designers to involve themselves in the supply of hardware.

The choice of a system designer will, again, depend on the type of database that the information provider wishes to place on CD-ROM. Clearly BRS and DEC would tend to be looked at first by companies planning to migrate online databases onto CD-ROM or to produce very large, complex databases on CD-ROM where there is a need for powerful, well-established free text retrieval software. However, for organisations looking to distribute smaller, simpler data files on CD-ROM in-house or to a specific set of users/customers, the smaller companies will be worth considering closely, if only because of the relatively low cost of their starter packs and the need to see how far one can get using a PC to create and load the database. Again, as time passes and the industry expands, individual companies will tend to specialise in particular application areas.

Due to shortage of space we will restrict ourselves here to considering the services currently being offered by two companies - BRS (Europe) and Office Workstations Ltd. (OWL) (the U.K. agents for Computer Access Company's Bluefish software and the Videotools Video Publisher system).

3.7.1 BRS (Europe)

BRS (Europe) share the view, outlined above, that while CD-ROM appears to be a perfect medium for the mass distribution of data, there are still some significant technical and commercial issues that need to be resolved before publishers can undertake large-scale CD-ROM publishing ventures and commit themselves to timetables, prices and performance specifications. They are, therefore, advocating that publishers undertake careful and realistic experimentation using a package of services that they have assembled based around their BRS/Search retrieval software. BRS claim that, for optical publishing, BRS/Search has three significant features.

Firstly, it is a free-text system, indexing the precise location of every word in the original text. This indexing, performed on a mainframe computer, means that all search queries are resolved by reference to highly structured files loaded on the CD-ROM. There is never any need to string search a document to resolve a query so the user is assured of good response times.

Secondly, BRS/Search is equipped with a menu-interface which allows publishers to develop their own user dialogue for particular information products. It is not necessary to produce another CD-ROM disc just to offer the user a new dialogue.

Thirdly, their so called print time formatting feature allows publishers to develop product-specific screen displays so again, it is not necessary to produce another disc simply to vary the display. Users can opt to make the screen resemble the frame of a microfiche or the page of a book.

BRS do not believe that publishers can accurately simulate products using a hard disk because this invariably limits the scale of the experiment in terms of database size and the number of users who can evaluate the product. Instead they are offering publishers the chance to produce a complete CD-ROM product, make replicates, evaluate them and, if necessary, adapt the menu interface and the screen format without changing the disc itself.

Specifically, BRS are inviting publishers to take part in what they call demonstration projects which comprise CD-ROM production, field trials and product development.

They can arrange for data capture if necessary and in co-operation with the publisher a BRS consultant will help with database design, considering the records that comprise the database and the fields within them and deciding which terms will be searchable and which will be just displayable.

The next stage is database conversion where the publisher's data is processed ready for input into the BRS load process.

The database load or inversion process takes the output from the database conversion process and extracts and stores every significant word in each field, along with a corresponding record number, field identifier and a location identifier for that word to produce an occurrence list. To load a large database involves a significant amount of computer processing and BRS state that on a large mainframe a database of 300 Mbytes can take 10 hours to load. Hence the relative efficiency of competing software products will be an important selling point.

The next stage is directory definition. Currently BRS, like any other disc producer, have to define the volume directory and ensure that the correct entries describing the files are inserted. While they can theoretically define any volume directory structure they also have to take into account the CD-ROM drive and operating system being used at the retrieval stage and develop the necessary device drivers to interpret the directory so data can be transferred to the search programme. As part of this stage of the process the files constituting the database are grouped together and, along with the directory, are reblocked into 2 Kbytes of data and output onto 1,600 bpi magnetic tape.

Now that the High Sierra Group working file format standard has been announced BRS is developing the necessary file structure creation programme that will allow them to follow the dictates of the standard and they consider that in future the directory definition and pre-mastering stages could effectively be merged.

The next stage currently is pre-mastering which is a standard procedure and has been outlined above. The significant point is that BRS will take responsibility for pre-mastering and for delivering the necessary tapes to the mastering facility which they will use to master and replicate the CD-ROM discs.

The next stage is a field trial and BRS will distribute the replicated discs to an agreed sample of prospective users to enable the publisher to conduct field trials. They will also provide the necessary retrieval hardware and software for users to test the performance of the discs. The typical workstation comprises a CD-ROM drive and controller, an interface card, a host computer with hard disk, an operating system, a device driver and BRS/Search software with its menu-interface subsystem and display-time formatting facility. Currently BRS/Search runs under a UNIX or UNIX-like operating system so for a single user microcomputer such as the IBM PC/XT they would recommend the PCIX operating system while for a multi-user microcomputer such as the IBM PC/AT they would recommend the XENIX operating system. For final, commercial exploitation of CD-ROM, BRS have also developed an MS-DOS/PC-DOS version of BRS/Search.

The final stage is product development. Once users have had an opportunity to evaluate the CD-ROM product they will be asked to suggest ways in which the system can be improved to meet their requirements more closely. BRS claim that the suggestions usually involve either amendments to the user dialogue or amendments to the display format. As described above, these can be catered for via the BRS/Search menu-interface sub-system or the display-time formatting facility without the need to produce a new disc.

The menu-interface subsystem is designed to enable customers to develop their own menu-driven end-user dialogue. It is possible for a customer to offer end-users a variety of dialogues - a database specific dialogue using the terminology of a particular application or market-place or a range of dialogues, each one tailored to the level of experience of the user. BRS supplies with the BRS/Search system a number of model interfaces which can be used as the basis for prototype dialogues but the main benefits are realised when a customer develops his own dialogue to meet particular market requirements. To date dialogues have been developed in a number of foreign languages, to simulate a number of online information services and to encourage direct end-user access to a very specialised database.

Display Time Formatting refers to the fact that while the records which comprise a database are stored in an internal BRS format for reasons of efficiency, on retrieval the records are re-formatted for display purposes and the re-formatting process has been designed to be very flexible and under customer control. Thus it is possible to develop display formats which match user or application requirements. While the layout of printed products has been defined according to traditions developed over many centuries, the rules which specify how a document should be displayed on a video terminal have yet to be developed. A video terminal has advantages and disadvantages and human factors need to be considered. There is a need for considerable experimentation in this field and hence for flexibility in the design and modification of screen formats.

BRS have already produced a number of prototype CD-ROM discs, most notably one they produced for the British Library holding 600,000 records from three bibliographic files. They are also working with a number of companies who are now developing commercial products.

3.7.2 Office Workstations Ltd.

Office Workstations Ltd. are an Edinburgh based company who have an agreement with Computer Access Corporation, suppliers of the Bluefish full text database management software in the U.S., and Videotools who market a product called the CD-Publisher, claimed to be the first IBM PC-based system for creating a CD-ROM database.

In the U.S., Computer Access Corporation and Videotools announced a joint offering of a CD-ROM Publishing Evaluation Kit at a price of just $9,800. Office Workstations Ltd. (OWL) were able to make the same package available in the U.K. at a price of ₤9,750.

The package included a Bluefish software and user license, use of the Videotools preparation service for user-processed data on a pure PC production path and pre-mastering and mastering of one master CD-ROM containing up to 50 Mbytes of user data plus production of 50 replicates by Philips Subsystems and Peripherals Inc. Also included in the price was a Philips CM 100 CD-ROM drive, card and driver software for use with an IBM PC. The Bluefish software is designed to run on an IBM PC or 100% compatible with 256K RAM running PC-DOS and offering floppy disk storage and this would have to be purchased if it was not already available.

Clearly there will be some severe limitations with such a package but it provides in-house users with a chance to prepare data on their own PCs and evaluate CD-ROM as an internal or external publishing medium. The Bluefish software is said to accommodate any ASCII text file and works entirely on an office IBM PC-XT-AT or compatible. Filters help remove unnecessary characters from word processing or typesetting files and Bluefish claim that one client, a major accounting company, took less than 12 hours to process an entire 50 Mbyte text file using Bluefish on an IBM PC.

The stages needed to produce a CD-ROM using the OWL package are:

a.   Collect data in machine readable form
b.   Process data on PC using Bluefish
c.   Deliver data to Office Workstations Ltd.
d.   Pre-mastering conducted by Office Workstations
e.   Mastering and replication of discs by Philips NV
f.   Delivery of CD-ROM discs to the user.

Currently, delivery times for pre-mastering and production range from 3-6 weeks.

A list of other companies offering CD-ROM production services can be found in Chapter Eight.

3.8   Costs of CD-ROM Production

It should be clear from the above description of all the stages involved in the production of CD-ROM databases that, while the total cost of creating a CD-ROM database can only be calculated on an individual basis, bearing in mind the size of the database, the retrieval software chosen, the timescale allowed and the number of replicates required, it is nevertheless possible to break the process down into stages and indicate prices for the standard elements of the process such as pre-mastering, disc mastering and replication. Clearly the current figures are high, reflecting the fact that most of the work is of a prototype nature, the software vendors are having to create and modify device drivers and file structure creation programs to suit individual requirements and the mastering facilities are extremely busy due to the demand for CDs.

Philips kindly supplied us with the following set of figures which can serve as a guide to current costs for mastering and replicating CD-ROM discs. The data preparation costs are very much average costs for preparing some 250 Mbytes of data, they do not include the cost of data capture or database design which would add substantially to the total.

What the figures do illustrate well, however, is that with CD-ROM, as with any publishing system, there are certain fixed costs such as the data preparation and the mastering which inevitably make small run publishing an expensive proposition. By contrast, there are relatively few on costs - just the replication cost - so once one gets into volumes of 250 or more discs the price per disc begins to look very attractive and the price per page of information distributed goes down to 0.02 pence.

(N.B. The figures given below are in pounds sterling and were approximate figures supplied to us by Philips for illustrative purposes. They do not necessarily reflect Philips' current prices for mastering and replication.)

COST OF CD-ROM PRODUCTION

Data preparation (250 Mbytes)	£9,250	£9,250	£9,250	£9,250	£9,250	£9,250	£9,250
Master disc	£2,750	£2,200	£2,200	£2,200	£2,200	£,2200	£2,200
Replica	£0	£27	£22	£16	£16	£14	£12
No. of discs	1	10	50	250	500	1000	1,500
Total price	£12,000	£11,720	£12,550	£15,450	£19,450	£25,450	£29,450

While it is extremely likely that these prices and those of other disc mastering and replication facilities will drop significantly over the next two years as more CD-ROM mastering and replication facilities come on stream and volumes increase, one should not get too carried away with predictions of $1 per replicate without looking carefully at the quality requirements of particular applications.

REFERENCES

1.   HAMILTON, C. (et al) Text retrieval: a directory of software. IIS. Gower
     Publishing Co. Ltd. ISBN 0566 03527 8.

2.   HENDLEY, A. M. Videodiscs, compact discs and digital optical disks: an
     introduction to the technologies and the systems and their potential for
     information storage, retrieval and dissemination. Cimtech Publication 23. 208
     pp. £24.00. ISBN 085267 245 4.

4.   WORKSTATION CONFIGURATIONS

In Chapter Three we described all the stages involved in designing and creating a
CD-ROM publication. We now switch our attention to the equally important area of
what hardware and software is needed for users to be able to access the data that has
been recorded on CD-ROM. Clearly there is a close relationship between the target
workstation and the design of the database and while, inevitably, given the serial
nature of a published report, we have to deal with one after the other, it should be
emphasised that currently, the publisher/software vendor and data preparer would all
have to make decisions about the target workstation before producing the CD-ROM
product.

Again, in Chapter Two, when dealing with standardisation and the High Sierra Group
proposed logical file format, we indicated that when this was widely adopted it would
leave the way free for a number of the key hardware/software elements of a
CD-ROM workstation to be standardised too. We shall try to indicate what effect
the High Sierra Group standard will have on workstation design and standardisation
and just how far standardisation at the workstation level can go and how far it will
take us toward the goal of disc and drive compatibility as enunciated by the
Information Industry Association.

Firstly, however, we must define what we mean by a CD-ROM workstation and look
at the main hardware and software elements.

4.1   Hardware elements of a CD-ROM workstation

As described in Chapter One, CD-ROM drives are computer peripherals and hence
can either be attached to an installed base of host computers or supplied complete
with a host computer as a dedicated CD-ROM workstation. There are three basic
hardware elements involved: the host computer, a physical interface and a CD-ROM
drive. While in future we may well see dedicated CD-ROM workstations, such as the
proposed CD-I players, designed specifically to play back data stored on CD-ROM,
the first generation of CD-ROM drives are being attached to existing host computers
and this raises some specific technical issues which are gradually being overcome.

Given that a CD-ROM drive has to be attached to a host computer, the next question
which the publisher or CD-ROM system provider had to ask was what computer
systems do we target. Factors to be borne in mind included the fact that most of the
early CD-ROM products were aimed at libraries and professional business users and if
CD-ROM was to compete with microfilm and online as a publishing medium then the
workstation costs had to be kept low. The obvious answer was to target the installed
base of IBM PCs and compatibles or, for more complex databases where powerful
retrieval software had to be supported by the host computer and hard disk storage
was required, the PC-XT/AT and compatibles. Hence the first generation of
CD-ROM based optical publishing systems will be based around the IBM PC/XT/AT
and compatibles and publishers/system providers will be looking to deliver CD-ROM
drives and interfaces as a package which the PC user can simply plug-in.

Looking to the future, the IBM PC range, its clones and future versions, will continue to form the basis of the majority of professional CD-ROM workstations but inevitably, as the market for CD-ROM systems develops and specialised applications emerge, CD-ROM drives will be attached to a very wide range of host computers from mainframes down to domestic microcomputers. Already mainframe and minicomputer suppliers are looking at distributing user manuals, documentation and software on CD-ROM and DEC has developed a CD-ROM workstation based around their MicroVAX supermicrocomputer range.

Similarly, looking at the large educational marketplace, two U.S. companies - Microtrends and Optical Media International - have developed interfaces between CD-ROM drives and the Apple Macintosh, IIe and II + microcomputers. Looking to the consumer marketplace, CD-ROM workstations based around Atari and other personal computers are also being developed. If one looks at specialised market areas such as CAD systems, desktop publishing and dedicated word processing systems one can see that the major suppliers in these fields will integrate CD-ROM drives with whatever host processors they use too. We cover the range of potential applications for CD-ROM systems in more detail in Chapter Five.

Having defined the host computers which CD-ROM drives are being interfaced to, we must now turn to the two other crucial hardware elements - the CD-ROM drives and the physical/logical interfaces. There are an increasing number of drives available and they are not completely standardised. The Philips/Sony Yellow Book standard provides for a high degree of standardisation in performance, as we have seen in Chapter One and as we describe below when reviewing currently available drives and interfaces. However, there are differences in the way in which the drives are addressed - some using a serial interface and some using a parallel interface - and they require and expect different control commands to operate them. In addition, the way in which the different drives acknowledge control commands, alert the host to errors, send time codes and transmit data do vary in detail. Hence, currently, as we shall see below, each drive supplier has to provide one or a number of physical/logical interfaces which, at one end, all link to his drive and at the other end link to one or a number of computer systems - one for each computer system.

In Europe, the majority of the drives currently in the field have been sourced from either Philips or Hitachi. In addition, the following companies have shown CD-ROM drives which range in status from available and in production to prototype: Sony, Denon, Panasonic, Sanyo, JVC and Toshiba. Many of these suppliers are developing a range of different drives including stand-alone and built-in versions and versions using different interfaces and controllers. The drive suppliers themselves offer interfaces to at least an IBM PC or compatible and are also beginning to offer SCSI interfaces. In addition, a number of third parties either offer one of the above drives under their own label with their own interfaces or simply market specific interfaces designed to link one drive with one computer and operating system. DEC offer the Philips CM 100 drive under their own label with interfaces to a range of DEC processors and the IBM PC and Reference Technology market the Hitachi CDR 1502S drive under their own label with their own proprietary interface to the IBM PC. This latter trend will, no doubt, continue.

Below we describe some of the drives currently on the market and indicate the interfaces which are supplied with them. As we have shown in Chapter One, many of the performance aspects of the drives are governed by the Philips/Sony Yellow Book standard so there is little variation but there is still scope for the various suppliers to compete in some areas. Some of the key areas where the drives compete with each other at present include the average and maximum access times offered; the size of the units; whether the drives are modified CD players intended for use as standalone units linked to PCs or whether they are compact units intended for integration into the form of a PC; what interfaces are supported and, of course, the price. The latter is difficult to specify at present because most drives will be supplied on an OEM basis by the suppliers and hence cost is a factor of volume. The high prices of CD-ROM drives and interfaces at present simply reflect the fact that, in the majority of cases, they are only selling in evaluation quantities.

4.1.1 CD-ROM drives currently available or in development

a. Philips currently offer three CD-ROM drives, all derived from consumer CD players and are said to be developing a new range of compact units designed for integration into the form of PCs. The three drives currently available are all stand-alone devices. One is a front-loading unit so, in the case of a PC workstation, it can sit on top of the processor and support the monitor. The other two are top-loading so they need to be positioned to the side of the processor.

The Philips CM 100 was the first Philips CD-ROM drive to be launched on the market - a top loading unit which offered a data transfer rate of 1.41 Mbits/sec, an average access speed of 1 sec and a maximum access speed of 2 secs. It was supplied with a serial interface and Philips offered their CM 155 host resident CD-ROM controller and cable to link the CM 100 to the IBM PC XT/AT and compatibles. The CM 155 controller can support two CM 100 drives if required and is supplied with a software driver that works with both PC-DOS and MS-DOS. It measures 115 x 320 x 267mm and weighs 5 kg. The combined price of the drive, cable and controller, in quantity one is £1,200.

In addition to the Philips interface to the IBM PC, DEC also offer the CM 100 with an interface to their MicroVAX II and VAXstation II systems, the MicroVAX I computer system and, more recently, the Rainbow 100 and IBM PC computers. The DEC CD Reader, comprising the player, interface and cable is currently priced at $2,195 in the U.S.

Recently, Philips have also introduced a new version of the CM 100 which they are calling CM 110 which is supplied with an SCSI controller card in the drive itself. The CM 110 can be used with the IBM PC if the PC is fitted with an SCSI host adapter interface card and the SCSI interface permits the daisy chaining of a number of peripherals such as CD-ROM drives to the same host adaptor interface card. The remaining features of the CM 110 are identical to those offered on the CM 100. Currently, an evaluation package comprising the CM 110 plus the SCSI controller, an IBM PC SCSI interface card, manual and software is priced at approximately £1,500.

The third Philips CD-ROM drive is the CDR X1000 which, again, is a modified CD player but which offers front-loading rather than top loading. It employs a standard SASI/SCSI I/O connector. The CDR X1000 employs a different casing to the CM 100 and measures 95 x 320 x 305mm. It is priced at £995 in quantity one.

b.   Hitachi offer two CD-ROM drives: the CDR 1502S and the CDR 2500. The CDR 1502S was the first drive they launched and, like the Philips CM 100, is basically a modified consumer CD player. It is a standalone unit with front loading. It offers a minimum data transfer rate of 153 KB/sec, average access times of 0.5 seconds and maximum access of 1 second. The CDR 1502S has an 8 bit parallel bus and was originally supplied with an interface card enabling it to be driven from an IBM PC or compatible. Recently, Hitachi, like Philips, have also announced the availability of an SCSI controller for the drive which would allow it to be connected to other computer systems. The PC card will still be provided with the SCSI controller available as an option in a standalone unit in a separate box with its own power supply. The new SCSI unit will be priced at an additional £600. The CDR 1502S measures 85 x 435 x 289mm and weighs approximately 5.9 kg. The unit, with the IBM PC interface is priced at £950 in quantity one. In addition, as noted above, Reference Technology sell the same unit, under their own label, with their own proprietary error-correction code and an interface card and connection cable that can be attached to an IBM PC or compatible for a total of $1,595 in the U.S.

The Hitachi CDR 2500 was launched after the 1502S and is designed as a compact, built-in CD-ROM drive that will fit into the form of a PC. The unit is, of course, front loading and offers the same performance as the 1502 with a minimum data transfer rate of 153 KB/sec, average access times of 0.5 sec and maximum access times of 1 second. Like the 1502S it will be supplied with an 8 bit parallel bus and an interface card enabling it to be driven from an IBM PC or compatible and, as an option, it will also be supplied with a standalone SCSI controller for connection to other PCs. The CDR 2500 measures 146 x 83 x 203 mm and weighs approximately 3 kg.

c.   Sony have shown three CD-ROM drives in the U.S.A. - the CDU 100, CDU 200 and CDU 5002. All three are supplied with their own system controllers and a 2 Kbyte buffer memory. The CDU 100 is a standalone, front-loading unit with its own power supply. It is supplied with two Sony 40-pin connectors and can be interfaced to the IBM PC or Sony PC and daisy chained to up to four more CD-ROM drives. The CDU 200 is also a standalone, front-loading unit which shares many of the same features as the CDU 100 but is supplied with an SASI bus and connector and one Sony 40-pin bus for connection to the CDU 100. Sony also supply two interface cards for these drives so they can be connected to the IBM PC/XT and compatibles.   The CDB-200 converts the 40-pin Sony bus to the IBM PC bus while the CDB-300 converts SASI to the IBM PC/XT bus. The CDU 5002 is a built-in type drive designed to be located in the form slide of a PC. Full details of the data transfer rates, access times and dimensions for the Sony drives were not available at the time of writing this report.

d.   Denon, a subsidiary of Nippon Columbia of Kawasaki, Japan, showed a CD-ROM drive called the DRD-550 and were said to be planning to distribute both standalone and built-in drives offering SCSI or PC bus interfaces. The units are not currently in production.

e.   Toshiba have also showed a prototype drive at a number of shows. Called the XM 2000 it is a standalone, front-loading unit with, it is claimed, extremely fast access times of less than half a second and a choice of IBM PC bus or SCSI interfaces. Toshiba were also quoting prices of under $500 for the unit in quantity but so far no firm dates have been given for availability.

f.   Panasonic have shown their SQ D-100 standalone drive and are said to be developing a half height built-in model as well. Like the Toshiba drive, the Panasonic drive offers fast access times of 0.6 seconds and offers a choice of IBM PC bus or SCSI interfaces.

g.   Sanyo and JVC have also shown prototype CD ROM drives but model numbers and specifications are not currently available.

To summarise, the Philips and Hitachi drives are currently available in the U.K. and Europe and drives from Sony, Toshiba and Panasonic can be expected soon. The drives which are in production are standalone units using the same casing as is used in CD players. Under development are full height and half height 5.25 inch drives for integration in PCs. These drives will eventually have to use the PC power supply.

Looking in more detail at the interfaces themselves, at their most basic they comprise a controller card plus a connecting cable that can be plugged into the microcomputer's main bus. In most cases the interface control software is actually supplied in the same cards. In some cases the interface contains additional RAM or error detection and correction firmware. Reference Technology have incorporated their own error detection and correction system into their interface to the Hitachi drive.

As an extreme case, Microtrends in the U.S. offer their Jonathan card which is a 32/16 bit coprocessor for the Apple IIe and II plus and is based on the Motorola 68000 microprocessor. 512 Kbytes of RAM are offered as standard with an option of up to 4 Mbytes and a standard clock speed of 10 MHz is used. The card is designed to extract as much performance as possible from the Motorola 68000 while satisfying the severe physical constraints imposed by the Apple IIe peripheral slot size. The card is then further expanded by the addition of plug-in expansion cards providing CD-ROM interfaces, SCSI controllers and multiple RS232 ports. The operating system on the Jonathan card is the OS 9 system from Microware which provides a portable, multi-tasking operating system and is the operating system being used in the proposed CD-I players. With the Jonathan card the underpowered Apple 6502 processor is transformed so that it can control a CD-ROM drive and Microtrends are understood to have developed interfaces to the Philips CM 100 and the Sony CD-ROM drives. However, the board alone, without the CD-ROM drive is priced at $1,495 so it is debatable whether educational users of Apple microcomputers would be able to justify the price at present.

Most of the early products, however, target the IBM PC installed base - specifying an IBM PC with the Intel 8086 microprocessor, the PC-DOS version 2.0 or later, 256 Kbytes of RAM, dual floppy disk drives and a monochrome display.

Two types of interface are common with the IBM PC. The de facto IBM PC bus interface can be used with a CD-ROM drive linked by a proprietary interface to a host resident controller card with a PC bus interface and with CD driver software. Alternatively, the SCSI standard I/O bus is used with the CD-ROM drive plus SCSI controller linked, optionally with other CD-ROM drives, via the standard I/O SCSI interface to an SCSI host adapter with a PC bus interface and SCSI driver software with a CD-ROM module.

A number of CD-ROM drive suppliers are now offering the Small Computer System Interface and SCSI may well emerge as a de facto standard in the medium term. However, it is inevitably a relatively complex interface and hence more expensive than a dedicated bus so at the IBM PC level the dedicated bus will no doubt continue to be used. Those with a technical interest in this topic are referred to an article by Warren expounding the case for using SCSI (1).

The key point for publishers and system providers to note at this stage is that physically, what is required to produce a CD-ROM workstation is a host computer, a suitable interface and a CD-ROM drive. If the host computer is an IBM PC then the system designer has a wide choice of drives and interfaces which he can either recommend to clients, lease or even sell as part of his package. If, however, another host computer is targeted such as the Apple Macintosh or DEC Rainbow then the choice is a good deal more limited at present.

In addition, since there is scope for incompatibility at the hardware level the onus is placed on the publisher to offer his clients a complete hardware package as an option to ensure that they can read the discs that he has produced.

4.2   Software elements of a CD-ROM workstation

Given that we are interfacing a CD-ROM drive to one of a range of popular computer systems, the first thing which must be taken into account is the fact that the installed base of computers will be using a range of operating systems and different versions of each operating system. These operating systems are a given and will partly determine the design of the device driver and file server software needed to control a CD-ROM drive and handle it as a peripheral of the host computer.

As pointed out in Chapter Three, with standard erasable magnetic disks, the construction of the volume directory and the maintenance of its entries is the responsibility of the computer system's operating system. With CD-ROMs, however, while it is necessary to construct a similar directory and insert the various statistics which describe the files to be loaded on the disc, this is not the responsibility of any operating system, nor can it be, given the CD-ROM's read only nature.

The next piece of software that has to be taken into account, therefore, is the origination software or the file structure creation programme that was used to structure the files and build the directory prior to mapping the database on CD-ROM. As the operating system cannot construct the volume directory and the file structure on the CD-ROM disc, either the operating system suppliers or the disc producer or the data preparation facility or the mastering facility have to define the volume directory and file structure or a standard volume and file format has to be agreed (the High Sierra Group proposal).

Currently there are a number of proprietary origination software packages on the market which were developed before the High Sierra Group working standard was proposed and which will continue to be used in certain circumstances in the future, where they are regarded as more effective or simpler to implement. One of the disadvantages with using non-standard file structures, however, is that the suppliers of each origination software package must also supply a corresponding file server software package (one for each operating system that he wants his system to run on) which understands the particular file structure employed and can translate requests from the application software (open file X and read X amount of data) into specific commands which the CD-ROM device driver can then interpret (go to sector number X and read off Y blocks of data).

If, in future, the High Sierra working volume and file structure standard is adopted by all data preparers, CD-ROM drive suppliers and operating system suppliers, then we are led to believe that each data preparer will be able to produce one origination software package or file structure creation programme which will structure the files and produce directories that meet the provisions of the HSG standard. He will then not need to worry about developing the necessary file server software for particular operating systems because the operating system suppliers will be able to produce one file server for their operating system which will then be usable with any CD-ROM disc produced to the HSG standard. All that will need to change is the device driver where different drivers will be required for different CD-ROM drives and interfaces and that will be catered for by the drive supplier or the operating system supplier.

The device driver is the next element we must consider. If an operating system does not currently offer a device driver for a CD-ROM drive then the drive supplier or the software supplier must provide a specific device driver for each of the CD-ROM drives on the market or as many as they wish to support. DEC's VMS operating system already has a device driver that can be used with the Philips CM 100 CD-ROM drive which they support. The device driver, as we have said, acts as a link between the file server software and the CD-ROM controller. When the application software requests a file to be opened and a set of data to be read, the file server accesses the directory on the CD-ROM, finds the physical location of the file and the requested data within the file and then commands the device driver to move the read head to a particular sector on the CD-ROM disc and read off X blocks or bytes of data. The device drivers will, for the foreseeable future, be operating system specific and drive specific although, of course, combination device drivers could be designed which served a number of operating systems and a number of drives.

The next key piece of software is, of course, the application software - in most cases the search arm of the retrieval software which was used to index the database and which now resides on the PC and allows the user to search the contents of the CD-ROM database.

The main areas of concern here are firstly, which operating systems the search software runs on and secondly, how much RAM and magnetic disk storage is required to support the search software package.

4.3   The current position

The current position is that there are a large number of drives on the market with a number of non-standard interfaces. Interfaces exist between all the drives and the IBM PC or compatibles and there are also interfaces between selected drives and the IBM PC XT/AT and compatibles, the DEC VAX and MicroVAX range, the DEC Rainbow and the Apple Macintosh, IIe and II plus.

A number of drive suppliers are beginning to offer an SCSI controller and interface which enable their drives to be connected to any host SCSI card.

The above computers and many more which will be connected to CD-ROMs in due course, support a number of operating systems. Currently, only one operating system offers a CD-ROM device driver - DEC's VMS - and that device driver is specifically for the Philips sourced CD-ROM drive. For VMS to work with any other CD-ROM drives, a new device driver will have to be written for each new drive. This is true for all operating systems. Every device driver is operating system specific and drive/interface specific.

In addition, when developing a device driver for Microsoft's MS-DOS or PC-DOS - the most popular operating systems in the IBM PC field - until recently the software vendor also had to supply additional software to overcome the 32 Mbytes file size limit of current versions of MS-DOS/PC-DOS. However, Microsoft has recently announced extensions to MS-DOS which will allow PC users running versions 3.1 and 3.2 of MS-DOS to read data from any CD-ROM disc that conforms to the final version of the HSG working standard.

The extensions allow the PC user to overcome the 32 Mbyte file size limitation in MS-DOS and access the full 550 Mbytes stored on a CD-ROM or even on multiple CD-ROMs. The Microsoft extension is claimed to make the CD-ROM drive appear like any other magnetic disk drive to the user and to the application software. The MS-DOS CDEX CD-ROM extension is classed as a separate product by Microsoft so a separate licence fee is required and Microsoft hope that it will be sold by the CD-ROM drive manufacturers.

As described in Chapter Three, currently data preparers and software suppliers have devised their own proprietary file structures and directories for CD-ROM and this means that they also have to write their own file server software for every operating system that they need to cater for. Hence, if a data preparer used his own file structure and wanted to make the disc usable on computers running a number of operating systems he would have to write a number of file server packages and a different data preparer using a different file structure would need to provide another different set of file server software packages.

In addition, if the publisher/system provider wanted to be able to offer, as part of his product, one CD-ROM drive and interface to users using all the above computers and operating systems, he would have to provide the physical interfaces from the drive to the range of computers and also device drivers for every operating system.

With all these variables and incompatibilities it is clearly not possible at the present time to produce a CD-ROM disc and expect it to be readable on a range of computer systems using a range of operating systems. In addition, there is almost no installed base of CD-ROM workstations to target at present - only an installed base of the above and other computers.

Up until now, therefore, in order to produce a CD-ROM product and get it into the marketplace at a reasonable price, even if it is only for evaluation, a publisher or CD-ROM system provider had to target a particular computer (normally the IBM PC in the configuration described above) plus a particular drive which comes with an interface to the IBM PC (e.g. the Philips drive in the U.K.). He also had to opt to use one or other of the file structures which were available and ensure that the necessary device driver was available to control the drive and the necessary file server software was available to support the chosen file structure. Finally, he would have to have ensured that the search software part of the retrieval software package he had used to index the database could run on the IBM PC.

Any attempt to widen the potential market for his CD-ROM product by enabling it to run on other computers and operating systems or on other drives linked to IBM PCs or other computers would have involved him in considerable expense developing new device and file server software for the other operating systems and possibly having to pay for new hardware interfaces to be developed between CD-ROM drives and other computers.

This situation does not inspire commercial publishers with the confidence to invest heavily in CD-ROM and commit themselves to CD-ROM products but it could be tolerated while publishers developed experimental products and enabled them to produce a certain number of bundled products where they provide a specific group of users with all the hardware and software necessary to access their CD-ROM.

More importantly, however, the situation does not inspire users with confidence as they face a situation where if they purchase a particular workstation configuration from one publisher they would probably not be able to read another publisher's CD-ROM disc on it.

To sum up the situation at present, with no adopted file structure standards and hence no standard file servers for operating systems it was hard to see CD-ROM ever being widely used outside of closed user groups. In-house users could define their own standards but CD-ROM systems would not appeal to publishers wishing to target end users in business, government and the educational field if they had to confine themselves to targeting one drive, computer and operating combination.

Fortunately, however, the emergence of the HSG working file format standard, as outlined in Chapter Two, looks set to usher in a second stage of CD-ROM workstation design where many of the above elements of a CD-ROM workstation can be standardised to allow publishers a wider range of workstations to aim their products at and users a wider range of discs which they can potentially access on their workstations.

Before going on to look at how future CD-ROM workstations can be standardised and streamlined, provided that the High Sierra Group file format is adopted, we must stop to outline the work of some of the pioneering companies who have gone ahead and developed their own CD-ROM workstations, usually as part of a complete CD-ROM hardware/software integration service where they will prepare data for distribution on CD-ROM, as outlined in Chapter Three and also provide a dedicated workstation using proprietary or third party hardware and software, all of which they will support.

As we pointed out in Chapter Three, this is the only practical approach to take in the early days of CD-ROM publishing in order to get a product out into the marketplace or test a product out. The two companies whose systems we have opted to look at in some detail are Reference Technology and Digital Equipment Corporation.

4.3.1 Reference Technology Inc.

Reference Technology offer what they call their CLASIX Series 500 DataDrive which is the Hitachi CDR-1502S drive, RT's proprietary error-correction code, and an interface card and connection cable that can be attached to an IBM PC or compatible for a total of $1,595. They can also supply a number of other hardware options including two multi-drive directors and two combined magnetic and CD-ROM drives. The MultiDrive Director MD-504 allows four 500 DataDrives to be connected to one IBM PC and costs $795, the MultiDrive Director MD-508 allows eight 500 DataDrives to be connected to one IBM PC and costs $900. The CLASIX DataDrive Plus Series 500/10 or 500/20 feature 10 or 20 MByte IOMEGA magnetic cartridge drives integrated with the 500 DataDrive.

Reference Technology also offer a number of data preparation services designed to help information providers produce CD-ROMs that can be played back on the RT workstation. TRIDECC is a pre-mastering system that can be used with both hybrid videodiscs and CD-ROMs. It comprises a minicomputer-based data preparation service which formats the data and adds RT's proprietary error correction coding for CD-ROM production. Their STA/F file system comprises a file manager and directory which contains an entry for each data file on the CLASIX CD-ROM. Using STA/F file the layout of data to be submitted to the disc mastering process can be speeded up by automatically generating the directory. STA/F file also removes the IBM PC-DOS file size limitation of 32 Mbytes and allows files up to 4 Gbytes to be supported. In effect, therefore, STA/F file is a proprietary CD-ROM file management system with origination software, a proprietary logical format and destination software.

RT also suppy retrieval software and database design services. Their STA/F Text System is a text retrieval software package which, when used with the Series 500 CD-ROM DataDrive allows users to perform free text or structured searches on IBM PC or compatible computers and retrieve documents that contain selected words, phrases or numbers. Their STA/F Key software is an access method that permits retrieval of information by multiple keys. When used with the Series 500 CD-ROM Datadrive the STA/F Key software allows direct retrieval of indexed records by any of up to 32,767 key fields.

4.3.2 Digital Equipment Corporation

Digital Equipment Corporation launched a fully integrated CD-ROM computer subsystem in 1985. It comprised a CD reader (a modified CM 100 from Philips), controller and cables and the choice of the new MicroVAX II and VAXstation II systems, the MicroVAX I computer system and, more recently, the Rainbow 100 and IBM PC computers. The CD reader, controller and cables were priced at $2,195 in the U.S. In addition, DEC announced their own Uni-file file format standard for CD-ROM and committed themselves to the provision of a CD-ROM application development service for information providers, based on the Uni-file format and the CD-ROM workstations listed above. For applications software, Digital have an agreement to use the MicroBASIS free text retrieval software from Battelle which runs on both MicroVMS and MS-DOS.

Hence DEC, like Reference Technology, offer workstation hardware and software and a range of data preparation services geared to producing CD-ROM databases that can be used on their workstations.

Both DEC and Reference Technology were represented on the High Sierra Group and are expected to adopt the High Sierra Group proposed file structure and support it in commercial publishing applications and other applications where the use of the standard is desirable while, at the same time, continuing to use their own proprietary file management systems in in-house publishing applications.

4.4 Future CD-ROM workstations

At the risk of being accused of crystal ball gazing, we would like to make a few tentative predictions concerning the design and price of future CD-ROM workstations. No-one currently knows what the next generation of professional microcomputers or personal microcomputers are going to look like so we will not discuss these but, based on what we have seen already in the first four chapters, it is possible to extract some trends and make some predictions of what future CD-ROM workstations will look like.

Physically, as we have said, current CD-ROM workstations comprise an existing host computer, an interface and a CD-ROM drive. Even at this level there is scope for considerable streamlining as half height 5.25 inch form CD-ROM drives become available which can be integrated into the PC and use the PC's own power supply. We also expect to see more CD-ROM drives using the SCSI interface and drives which offer faster average access times. In addition Philips are predicting multi-disc handling devices, of the type which already exist for domestic CD players, which will allow six or more CD-ROMs to be handled automatically and loaded into one CD-ROM drive. Clearly new interfaces would be needed to cater for such systems but Reference Technology have already proved this to be practical with their MultiDrive units.

One further development, which we hinted at above, will be the development of dedicated CD-ROM workstations which, like the proposed CD-I players, will incorporate a CD-ROM drive plus a microprocessor and will be aimed at non-computer users where the emphasis is on simplicity of use with limited keypad or mouse type operation.

Looking to the software side, we expect the High Sierra Group working standard to have a significant impact if, as appears likely, it is widely adopted as an industry standard over the next 6-12 months. The existence of a file format standard will lead to a greater confidence in the industry and take some of the risk element away from CD-ROM publishing. At the workstation level it should mean that only one file server will be needed for each operating system or at least one for the High Sierra Group standard and one for the operating system suppliers proprietary structure (e.g. DEC's Uni-File).

In future, new versions of personal computer and indeed, all computer operating systems will be designed to support very high density read only, write once and erasable storage media and Microsoft have already developed an extension to MS-DOS 3.1 and 3.2 that will support files extending to several Gbytes.

We also expect to see device drivers developed for all the main drives on the market and all the main operating systems so it will be possible, as cheaper and higher performance CD-ROM drives become available, for system providers or publishers to switch from one drive to another without having to rewrite device drivers themselves.

Hence, in a relatively short period of time (12-24 months), it should no longer be necessary for publishers/information providers to either provide or specify the use of specific drives, interfaces, computers, operating systems or file structures. It will be sufficient to employ the High Sierra Group file structure and several versions of a retrieval software package that can be run on most of the common operating systems on most of the common desktop computers currently available.

All the above points should, in our view, have a positive effect both in terms of market acceptance of CD-ROM publishing systems and also, not unrelatedly, in terms of the cost of future CD-ROM workstations. Currently, as we have seen above, typical costs for a CD-ROM drive and the necessary interface to an IBM PC range from £1,200-£2,200. To this would have to be added the price of an IBM PC or any other host computer to provide a true workstation cost of approximately £4,000 which is still very high when comparing CD-ROM to microfilm or paper-based publishing systems. It is not so high when comparing CD-ROM to online systems where many users would already have the necessary IBM PC.

In future, as volumes grow and the file format standard is adopted, we would expect to see the price of the drive and interface combination drop quite rapidly to £500 and some even predict an eventual price of £200-£250. Similarly, the price of IBM PCs and compatibles is set to fall to below £500 with the latest Amstrad machine - providing a possible conventional CD-ROM workstation cost of well under £1,000 in the next two years.

If one looks at the CD-I development then we could well see such dedicated players selling for approximately £300-400 provided the required volume is there. Clearly, for every drop in price of the CD-ROM workstation a larger potential marketplace appears, particularly in the consumer and educational fields. In the professional markets, however, the hardware costs are not always the key factors. Many users will want CD-ROM workstations supplied from one source with good service and support facilities and will be prepared to pay a premium for this service. CD-ROM workstations, as indeed CD-ROM applications, will range from sophisticated, expensive workstations targeted at senior professionals to low cost kit systems aimed at computer hobbyists and some parts of the consumer and educational sector. The type of workstation configuration supplied will obviously depend, in the final analysis, on the main application areas where CD-ROM systems are used and we must now turn to the applications.

References

1. WARREN, C. SCSI Bus eases device integration. CD-ROM: the new papyrus, pp 85-90. Microsoft Press. ISBN 091484 575 6.

5. APPLICATIONS FOR CD-ROM AS A PUBLISHING MEDIUM

5.1 CD-ROM - the solution is coming now where are the problems?

In the first four chapters of this report we have defined what a CD-ROM is, analysed the key areas which have been or are becoming standardised, outlined all the stages involved in preparing data for distribution on CD-ROM and, finally, described the type of workstations that will be needed to access data stored on CD-ROMs. Overall, we have explained how, over the next few years, Compact Disc Read Only Memory systems, when linked to personal computers, could evolve into standardised, high density, low cost, reliable data distribution media, effectively offering publishers of all kinds yet another distribution channel alongside online, microfilm or paper systems.

What we aim to do in this and the following two chapters is look at the why, when, who and how many of CD-ROM publishing. Is CD-ROM just a solution looking for a problem? Will it replace existing media or will it find its own unique niche in the ever growing information world and complement rather than replace existing media? Specifically, we shall look at those traditional areas of publishing where CD-ROM appears to have a role and at those publishers/system providers who have already shown prototype or commercial CD-ROM publishing systems. We shall also look at some new types of publications which simply were not viable before the emergence of CD-ROM but which may well become viable, as CD-ROM takes off and costs come down, and fill real gaps in the information marketplace. Having defined the application areas, we will then go on to compare CD-ROM with optical and more traditional publishing media (e.g. paper, microfilm and magnetic media).

5.1.1 Trends in computing and publishing

Before dividing up the world of publishing and assessing CD-ROM's role in each specific application area, we must briefly look at some of the trends in the publishing and computer world which could either promote or restrict the acceptance of CD-ROM and other read only optical media as publishing media and then summarise the key facts that will influence CD-ROM's performance in each particular area of publishing.

The first key trend in the office automation and publishing markets and, to a lesser degree, the educational and consumer marketplace, has been the rapid growth in the use of personal computers and the consequent decline in the price of such units. It is widely predicted that by 1990 there will be some 40 million personal computers installed worldwide and the price of the basic IBM PC and compatibles, at the time of writing this report, had just dropped to a staggering £399 with the introduction of the Amstrad PC range. By 1990 the actual price of a PC will clearly be a very minor consideration, even in high volume applications.

The widespread availability of PCs has fostered, and will increasingly foster, the demand for electronic information products where data is searchable and accessible from a desktop rather than by rifling through desk drawers or reels of microfilm. There will be a demand for ever more source material to be keyboarded or OCR scanned so that the full text can be held online and searched on a free text basis and an increasing proportion of the data received by companies, libraries and government departments will be in electronic form via electronic publication services or via electronic mail from other departments and suppliers.

These two developments will create a tremendous demand for data storage facilities, both write once and erasable, for building up databases in-house and downloading data from electronic databases. Sensing this demand, many companies are developing high density write once and erasable digital optical disk storage units which will attach to PCs, as described in Chapter One.

The optical publishing proponents claim that there will also be a growing demand for read only storage media so that PC users can purchase published databases and reference works on low cost read only media and then access them locally on their PCs. Optical read only systems, as described in Chapter One, would meet this requirement and of those CD-ROM is tipped as the most promising of the optical read only devices.

However, this claim needs a little consideration as, at first sight, it appears to go against a current trend in electronic publishing and the provision of library and information services within companies and public sector organisations. That trend, over the past ten years, has been towards the centralised provision of bibliographic data via online database enquiry systems and the centralised provision of full text information via national or regional interlibrary loan services.

Twenty years ago, bibliographic data was supplied exclusively in hardcopy form and libraries took out subscriptions to such services as Chemical Abstracts, Engineering Index and the British National Bibliography and received weekly, monthly, quarterly and yearly sets of printed listings. Such lists were invariably out of date and had to be ordered and filed and paid for whether they were heavily used or not. The result was that when these databases were made available online and the necessary telecommunications and terminals arrived, many libraries discarded their hardcopy listings and relied instead on an online service where the data was more up-to-date and they only paid for what they used.

In addition, once the concept of online database retrieval became established, many publishers of directories and financial information services also began to offer online services instead of printed services and many of these were used by professional end users rather than by trained librarians or information officers. Hence we had a trend away from buying and storing information locally in hardcopy form, in case it was needed, towards using external online information services where you only paid when you needed the information and you were sure that you were accessing the most up-to-date version of the database.

With CD-ROM information products, although the data is in coded form and hence is searchable on a computer, libraries and many of the professional end users who currently access external databases online are going to be asked to go back and pay once for the privilege of holding a complete database locally - just as they were previously asked to pay once for hardcopy products and the database on CD-ROM could be as much as 8 weeks out-of-date just as the printed products were out of date by the time they reached the user. The worry must be that some users will see this as a retrograde step and will not install CD-ROM hardware.

In practice, the above is too simple an analysis, ignoring such factors as the cost of online services, telecommunication charges and user convenience and giving the impression that online and CD-ROM are two options that a user must choose between. This is not the case and as we go on to look at some of the main applications where CD-ROM will be used we will see that in some cases it will complement online services, in others it will challenge paper publications and in others it will usher in totally new publications and services that could not have been provided online or on paper. We would summarise the above by saying that there is a vast and ever growing number of PC users worldwide which represents an enormous potential market for CD-ROM based publishing systems. The question that has to be asked is what publications are best distributed to those PC users on CD-ROM for local access and what are best made available online via ever improving telecommunications facilities?

5.1.2 Advantages and disadvantages of CD-ROM as a publishing medium

We must now close this introductory section by summarising the main advantages and disadvantages of CD-ROM as a publishing medium. The advantages of CD-ROM include:

a.   Its high storage capacity (550 Mbytes or some 200,000 pages of coded text)

b.   The fact that it is based on an established mass produced audio medium and hence drive and media costs can be kept low and the technology is proven

c.   The fact that the computer and information industry have co-operated to develop a file format standard which should enable CD-ROMs designed to that standard to be read by a range of different operating systems running on different computers linked to different CD-ROM drives

d.   The fact that the economics of CD-ROM publishing mirror CD music publishing, book publishing and newspaper publishing - the more you can sell the lower the per unit production costs - hence the most popular material can be sold very cheaply and still be very profitable to the publishers.

The limitations are:

a.   Currently, the data preparation, pre-mastering, mastering, replication, checking, packaging and distribution cycle is a complex one and turnaround times are inevitably long. No publisher at present is planning for more than a monthly update cycle and that will mean that, in many cases, material published on CD-ROM could be 8 weeks old by the time it is available.

b.   The CD-ROM is a computer peripheral and the PC market is extremely volatile and competitive. While this leads to impressive cost reductions in hardware and hence widens the market for CD-ROM products it can also pose the publisher certain problems as the computer and software companies update operating systems and hardware ever more rapidly in order to gain competitive advantage.

c.   CD-ROM, being based on the CD audio CLV format, offers slow access times and hence databases and retrieval software have to be designed to overcome this limitation.

d.   CD-ROM may be challenged, in future, by other read only memory formats such as OROM (see Chapter Seven) with its 5.25 inch diameter and fast access CAV format, which will be compatible with 5.25 inch write once and erasable optical disk systems.

e.   The final limitation concerns the question of graphics on CD-ROM. So far in this report we have not covered graphics in any detail. Most of the current prototype CD-ROM systems deal only with coded textual material and in describing how data can be prepared for CD-ROM publishing we limited ourselves to alphanumeric data. Clearly, as the industry develops, graphics of all kinds will be recorded on CD-ROM and many of the potential applications for CD-ROM which we describe in this chapter assume that both graphics and data can be recorded on CD-ROM. As described in Chapter Two, the High Sierra Group working standard does not in any way preclude the recording of graphics on CD-ROM but, equally, it does not specify how graphics should be recorded on CD-ROM and a lot of work needs to be done to investigate such questions as resolution, standards, workstation design, storage requirements, compression and decompression and the cost implications of handling graphics on CD-ROM.

The term graphics also covers a very wide range of different graphic material including computer generated graphics (CAD symbols, business graphics and chemical structures), raster scanned or facsimile type images where a page of handwritten text, a diagram or photograph is scanned via a CCD array, digitised and stored as a digital bit map and video images where a picture, photograph or slide is captured on a video camera and either an analogue or a digital image of the original can be stored in analogue or digital form on videotape, videodisc, CD-ROM or CD-I and retrieved and displayed on a video screen.

Different applications will require the use of one or more of these graphics and the technical requirements for handling each type of graphic material will be different and will have considerable implications on the design and cost of the user's retrieval workstation and the CD-ROM database itself. The simplest applications cover alphanumeric data only (these include the majority of the first applications) and these are the ones which we have described in the proceeding chapters and on which we have based our costings for data preparation and end user workstations the majority of the first applications,. One has to start somewhere with any new technology and we, and most of the suppliers, have started by excluding graphics.

The second stage is the incorporation of computer graphics. Here the main issues relate to standards and unless extremely sophisticated CAD graphics are required, the incorporation of computer graphics in CD-ROM information products should not have a significant impact on the design and cost of the user's retrieval terminals. Just as one can see chemical symbols on chemical databases today so one will also see chemical symbols, graphs and diagrams on CD-ROM databases.

Moving onto raster scanned images, here we feel that the technical problems involved in handling raster scanned images on CD-ROM and the implications in terms of the storage capacity of the CD-ROM discs and the design of the workstations have not been adequately stressed or explained in books or articles to date. As an example, a number of industry commentators have glibly talked of CD-ROM as a replacement for academic or technical microform publishing where images of back runs of periodicals or collections of books, photographs, works of art and manuscripts are recorded onto microfilm and copies of the film sold to libraries and other organisations. To use CD-ROM in these applications at present would prove prohibitively expensive. First the page images would have to be raster scanned using CCD array scanners that operate more slowly than microfilm. Secondly, the images would need to be compressed, transferred from magnetic disk onto tape and from there onto a master CD-ROM. Then replicate CD-ROMs would be distributed to end users and to access the images and see a complete page on the screen, the users would require very high resolution terminals with decompression hardware and page RAM stores and laser printers for hard copy. Such a workstation would inevitably be a non-standard specialised product at the moment so, in addition to the high cost, a further problem would be that libraries would not be able to purchase one high resolution workstation to access all image material on CD-ROM, they might need to buy a number from different suppliers to access all the image material that would be made available on CD-ROMs.

Assuming that lower cost workstations could be developed, and of course they will be in time, once the textual applications of CD-ROM have taken off and costs have come down, there is still the question of storage capacity to contend with. As pointed out in Chapter One, while a CD-ROM can store up to 200,000 pages of coded text, the same CD-ROM can only currently store approximately 6,000-10,000 A4 page images scanned at 200 dots per inch (according to the CCITT Group 3 standard) and compressed at approximately 10:1. No doubt in time more efficient compression ratios will be used but these are unlikely to be standard ratios so at present all one can say is that it looks as though it will be a very long time before CD-ROM challenges traditional microform publishing for the distribution of vast collections of images on a cost basis.

Finally, careful study will reveal to publishers that most of the scholarly material purchased on microfilm by libraries and research centres is not heavily used. Because the cost per frame or per document is relatively low, libraries purchase vast collections on microfilm to help complete the balance of their collections and usually there is a lot of redundant or duplicated material in the collection which is almost never referred to.

Given this last factor it would be very difficult to justify spending any more money to obtain low usage image material on CD-ROM rather than on microfilm, even if the CD-ROM system was much easier to use. We compare source document microfilm and computer output microfilm with CD-ROM in more detail in Chapter Six. All we wish to point out here is that while, in future, raster scanned images will be made available on CD-ROM, initially it will be the minimum number required to illustrate a journal article or textbook or else it will be images of extremely valuable, high use material where the publisher can be sure of selling lots of copies of the CD-ROMs and the user finds the image data to be so valuable that he is prepared to pay a premium for the workstation required to access it.

Thirdly, when talking of video images we must make the point again that currently CD-ROM can only be used to store static still frame video images because the CD-ROM drive does not revolve quickly enough to permit moving images to be transferred continuously from the disc and displayed on a video screen. If high quality moving video is required then currently videodiscs are the preferred medium. CD-I, the new Philips/Sony consumer standard, allows video and audio information to be recorded on CD-ROM alongside text and data but even here the transfer rates from the disc to the display only support still frame video or animated sequences, full quality moving video is still not attainable with CD-I.

The problems involved in handling graphics and some of the efforts being made to overcome them will be touched upon again in this chapter where they are crucial to the success of a particular application. We will also deal with them in the next two chapters when comparing CD-ROM with other optical publishing media and more traditional publishing media.

5.2 Defining what we mean by publishing

In looking at the publishing applications for CD-ROM, we do not want to get into competition with the main market survey companies and start talking about how many million drives will be installed by 1990 or what the value of CD-ROM based information products will be by 1992. We would point readers who want detailed market predictions to the many reports currently available from companies such as Link Resources, Rothchild Consultants, Frost & Sullivan and Diversified Data Resources (1-4). What we do want to do is, firstly, come up with a working definition of what publishing encompasses and break the field down by types of publications and by application areas and then, secondly, assess the applicability of CD-ROM to each and indicate ways in which the availability of CD-ROM could change the manner in which various types of publication are distributed and the ways in which various applications are served by the publishing industry.

For convenience we have broken the publishing field up into four application areas: the professional market, the library market, the educational market and the domestic market. The professional market here includes all publications either originated or purchased and used by businesses and public sector institutions. The library market could be subsumed within the educational market but it is one which has been specifically targeted by the pioneers of CD-ROM publications and hence needs separate attention. The education and domestic consumer market are related and one of the main issues there is the degree to which CD-ROM or CD-I systems are used at school or in the home.

We have further divided the professional marketplace into three categories of publishing. The first is 'in-house' or 'corporate publishing', the second is 'technical publishing' and the third and more traditional category is 'commercial publishing' where the publisher identifies a market for a particular publication or information service and then produces, organises and stores it, makes it available in the most appropriate form and then proceeds to market it via established channels to his perceived market. This area of commercial publishing is then further subdivided by the type of publication or the subject area. Categories we have chosen include software distribution, graphic databases, database publishing, specialised information services, reference works and facsimile images of documents.

It has been our impression, reading the literature, attending conferences and talking with suppliers and end users that the third category of publishing, 'commercial publishing' is seen as the major application area for CD-ROM publishing. While we see CD-ROM having a major role in this area, we feel that CD-ROM is best suited to the technical publishing and in-house publishing environment and, in the short term, there could prove to be far less barriers to acceptance in these two relatively controlled environments.

5.3   The professional market

As defined above, we will look in this section at the potential applications for CD-ROM publications in commercial and public sector organisations, looking first at in-house publishing applications, then technical publishing applications and finally commercial publishing applications.

5.3.1 In-house publishing

By in-house or corporate publishing systems, we mean systems for capturing, organising, storing and disseminating information within a company or public sector body. Today this normally involves the use of word processing systems and/or in-house reprographic units or commercial print shops to produce and print reports, telephone directories, sets of statistics, minutes of meetings, technical reports and sales forecasts which are then distributed to a list of people within the organisation who need to receive that information. In addition numerous copies are kept on file for various purposes and usually microfilmed at some stage in their life. While paper is still the most popular medium for distributing this in-house information, many organisations also use computer output microfiche and online electronic distribution via PC networks and private viewdata systems. Ever increasing amounts of the information are being produced on word processors or microcomputers and with desktop publishing systems being introduced which can handle both text and graphics and enable users to carry out sophisticated page make-up functions, there will be increasing pressure to store and disseminate the resulting internal publications electronically rather than print them out and incur heavy consumable costs.

Against this background, a number of major office automation, computer and reprographic companies are evaluating where CD-ROM can fit into future in-house electronic publishing systems and several are already offering large clients the opportunity to experiment with CD-ROM publishing systems in-house. In the forefront of such companies are Digital Equipment Corporation who are offering their existing customers the opportunity to experiment with CD-ROM based in-house systems and Reference Technology in the U.S.A. who have recently announced a teaming agreement with Xerox Corporation to market CD-ROM systems for in-house information distribution. According to Richard Goldner, Marketing Manager, Standard Product Systems for Xerox Special Information Systems, "Reference Technology's expertise in CD-ROM, which includes hardware, fast search software and comprehensive data preparation services, complements Xerox's advanced workstations, laser printers and broad systems integration capability".

For Reference Technology, Ronald Maierhofer, Vice President of Sales and Marketing said "We're excited about teaming with Xerox, the industry leader in this venture. Together we're now positioned to address the growing demand within government agencies and large corporations and take advantage of the benefits of CD-ROM for information distribution".

In a similar move, Reference Technology have also signed a major sales agreement to supply CD-ROM products and services to Capital Systems Inc., a government contractor/system integrator in the Washington DC area. According to Howard Ulep, President of Capital Systems "Our customers are beginning to demand the ability to distribute information on read-only optical discs. We sought out Reference Technology because we knew they were the industry leader in government applications development. We determined that they were uniquely able to provide a full range of products and services including hardware, software and data preparation in both CD-ROM and 12 inch disc formats". According to Stephen Snyder of Reference Technology "CD-ROM applications are rapidly growing in popularity among government agencies, especially within the Department of Defence. Distribution of technical documentation and print-on-demand systems are examples of personal computer-based applications where these agencies can accomplish their data management missions at significant cost savings".

Recently, at the AIIM show in San Francisco, Laserdata, a pioneer in CD-ROM and optical disk filing systems, showed an interesting prototype IBM PC compatible electronic page imaging system called Laserview. There are two main elements of the system: a filing system and a retrieval workstation.

The filing system comprises an IBM PC, XT, AT or compatible, a 300 dpi scanner, digital compression and decompression hardware, a high resolution, MS-DOS compatible monitor, a laser printer which supports standard printer output in addition to hard copy of the page images, write once optical discs for storing the page image databases, a complete package of indexing and retrieval software and, optionally, a 9 track magnetic tape drive used for data pre-mastering if the database being created on the filing system is to be distributed on CD-ROM or network interface hardware if the page images are to be networked. The filing system is a combination production and retrieval station which allows the user to develop databases of tens of thousands of page images.

The Retrieval Workstation is intended for applications which require distribution, viewing and printing of electronic page images. It can accept networked data from the filing system or the page images can be accessed from write once optical disks or CD-ROMs. The workstation comprises an IBM PC fitted with decompression, monitor control and printer control hardware, a high resolution monitor which displays an entire 8.5 x 11 inch page at once, a table top laser printer and a CD-ROM drive or networking hardware. The Laserview filing system is priced at under $40,000 in the U.S. and the Retrieval Workstation at under $15,000.

What the Laserview system, and many others currently under development, aim to offer is the ability to create mixed mode image and coded text documents, store them on write once optical disk locally and then make them available to remote users either via a network system or by serially copying the write once optical disks and distributing them to other users with retrieval workstations or, if there are a sufficient numbers of users, by mastering a CD-ROM and distributing copies to the end users. The Laserview system accepts high resolution raster scanned images and the displays used are high resolution 2,400 x 1,575 lines so the costs are inevitably high, as explained above, but the Laserview system demonstrates well, on a small scale, the potential options that will be open to users of in-house electronic publishing systems in future.

When looking briefly at industry trends we said that in the commercial publishing and library area the trend was towards the use of centralised electronic information services and CD-ROM, though an electronic storage medium, was bucking that trend by trying to get users to return to the local delivery of physical packages of information. So too, in in-house publishing systems, there will be a conflict between those who advocate putting all corporate information up on the mainframe and making it available to users via PCs linked on a network and those who advocate that individual departments should download their information onto CD-ROM and distribute it to those users who really need it. The advantages of using CD-ROM are that there will be no contention, as users seek time on the mainframe, response times will be quicker, users can spend as long as they like accessing the CD-ROM database and have access to the entire 550 Mbytes and not just that portion which they have called for and stored locally on a magnetic disk buffer, the retrieval software used for specific CD-ROMs can be geared specifically to the needs of the users and the data provided on the CD-ROMs can be packaged according to the requirements of the specific targeted users.

Some of the disadvantages of CD-ROM in such in-house applications are as follows:

a.   The main one, as we have described in Chapter One, is the lengthy turnaround times currently associated with CD-ROM and the fact that corporate users will have to send data outside to get discs mastered and replicated. While, on small runs, 3M and others are offering turnaround times of three days, such a service carries a high premium and normal turnaround times are closer to two weeks. In addition, for the short term, there is a chronic shortage of CD-ROM mastering and replication facilities.

b.   Allied to this are the skills and resources needed to convert a database into a form where it can be easily updated and reissued on a quarterly or monthly cycle on CD-ROM. The deadlines imposed by the CD-ROM production cycle will impose stricter disciplines on the staff responsible for creating, amending and updating the corporate databases than was previously the case with printed or microform publications and there will be a need for some major reassessment of the ways in which databases are structured in order to make them as flexible and as easily updatable as possible. Most users today still have their information in page or image form and the investment required to convert it into a versatile database format is proving a major disincentive to their adoption of CD-ROM publishing solutions.

c.   There is the high one-time cost of producing the master CD-ROM which would have to be absorbed over what could be, in many applications, a relatively low number of copies of the discs. Again, this figure will drop as volumes increase and more mastering and replication facilities come on stream.

d.   There is the high one-time cost of CD-ROM drives. At present drives from DEC and Reference Technology are priced at approximately $1,500-2,000 and if high resolution terminals are required for image display then, as we have seen with the Laserview system, the cost of a workstation rises significantly.

e.   Lastly, there is the timescale and cost involved in implementing an in-house CD-ROM publishing infrastructure. Again, as the major companies move into this area, procedures will be simplified and costs will come down but at present, installing a medium size in-house CD-ROM distribution system could cost close to $500,000, as described in an excellent paper given by Pete Rudnicky of Digital Equipment Corporation at the 1985 Videodisc, Optical Disk and CD-ROM Conference organised by Meckler Publishing (5).

According to Rudnicky the issues which need to be resolved include finding proper search and retrieval software, how to meet quarterly manufacturing cycles and determining how to accommodate the end user's requirements. The assumptions made in the study were that the CD-ROM drives were being added to existing host computer systems, that the application was full text only and that the company had an organisational need to use CD-ROM in-house to solve information distribution problems, achieve cost savings over existing methods, inprove communications and ultimately improve end user productivity.

In terms of timescale and cost, Rudnicky allowed 25 weeks for technology evaluation at a cost of $15,000, 13 weeks for field testing some five CD-ROM drives at a cost of $12,000, one year for initial implementation which involved producing the database, creating four masters at quarterly intervals, replicating 50 copies of each of the four masters, purchasing 50 CD readers and implementing and starting up the system at a cost of $195,500. A second year saw the expanded implementation which included four further updates of the database, mastering four more discs and producing 100 replicates of each and purchasing and installing a further 50 CD-ROM readers at a total cost of $176,500. The third year was described as steady state where the 100 CD-ROM readers are installed and in use and all that requires to be done is the production of four more updates of the database and maintenance of the readers at a cost of $62,000.

Overall the project, which resulted in the installation of 100 CD-ROM players and the production of one 200 Mbyte CD-ROM database with quarterly updates, cost a total of $461,000. Clearly this is a considerable amount of money and indicates that we are still some way off from seeing massive corporate wide networks of CD-ROM drives being installed but if one considers that close to 50% of that total represents the purchase price and maintenance cost of the readers and that the price of CD-ROM readers is likely to fall from $2,000 to about $500 in the next two to three years then one can see how such systems could well prove attractive to organisations who have already spent millions of dollars installing computer networks and now want to make full use of them. We look at the impact that such CD-ROM systems could have on in-house use of computer output microfiche in Chapter Six and compare CD-ROM with WORM disks for data distribution in Chapter Seven.

5.3.2 Technical publishing

Technical publishing systems will inevitably overlap somewhat with the in-house systems we have been describing above and may be run in-house in some cases. Typically, they involve the capture, manipulation, storage and dissemination of technical documentation: parts lists, instruction manuals, specifications, book order lists, standards, pricing information, maintenance schedules, timetables and statistics of all kinds. One significant difference between technical publishing and in-house publishing systems, however, is that usually the information has to be distributed outside the originating organisation to a controlled set of users such as clients, suppliers, dealers, distributors, retailers or branch offices.

A specific example would be car manufacturers such as Ford, Austin Rover and General Motors who produce and send out parts catalogues and price lists on microfiche on a monthly or quarterly basis to their many thousands of dealers. Technical publishing is, therefore, closer to traditional commercial publishing than in-house publishing in that the technical publisher is usually aiming at an external audience. However, that audience, in the case of dealers, is usally a captive one and can be given or instructed to purchase the hardware and software needed to access the published information - a microfiche reader or a specific computer terminal or in future, perhaps, a CD-ROM drive linked to a specific computer.

Like the in-house user the technical publisher currently has the option of distributing information on paper, microfiche or online via an electronic distribution network. As the information usually needs to be kept more up-to-date than with in-house publications there has tended to be a greater use of computer output microfiche and online systems here. There is a need to handle computer graphics in the parts catalogue application which has necessitated the use of more sophisticated and hence expensive graphic COM recorders such as the Hell Digiset unit employed by Bemrose at Derby to produce the master microfiche for Ford's catalogues.

It is clearly going to be very difficult for CD-ROM to beat microfiche on cost grounds alone. A standard microfiche reader, of the type used by most dealers, will not cost more than £200-300 to purchase and the microfiche, which are copied at high speed using contact photographic methods have low mastering and replication costs. The only way CD-ROM can be justified at this stage is by stressing the value added features which it can bring and these are significant in the parts catalogue area.

Firstly, there is the ease of use aspect. Currently dealers have to consult an index, extract the relevant fiche, load it in a reader, go to the index frame, check the frame number required, go to the frame and search for the part number on the screen. This can take some time and be very inconvenient if there is a considerable queue of people. With CD-ROM there would be a series of menu screens and the user could search the catalogue intelligently and interactively, asking for a particular part. In addition, as the CD-ROM would be controlled by a computer system, once the part had been identified, one key stroke could ascertain its current price and whether it is in stock locally and if it is not in stock another key stroke could order the part and adjust stock totals. All transactions and look-ups would be monitored and reported on by the system so checks could be made on what spares were most in demand and which were never used, allowing dealers to improve their stock-keeping and reduce their overheads and customers would receive a faster, more accurate response to their enquiries. Not too far into the future, the dealer's PC plus CD-ROM drive could be left switched on when the showroom was shut and customers could access the stock list online and check availability of parts.

A number of suppliers of CD-ROM based systems are targeting the parts catalogue and general technical publishing area. At the AIIM Show in San Francisco in May 1986, NCR, a leading supplier of computer output microfiche systems who developed and promoted the use of high density ultrafiche systems in the 1960s and 70s, were showing prototype CD-ROM workstations and prototype CD-ROM based part catalogue applications and were offering to produce experimental systems with potential customers of such systems. Their Systemedia Group is working with a number of distributors of parts information to develop new electronic publishing systems. They claim that their automated parts system will offer many advantages over microfiche or printed parts catalogues including faster access to parts information; multiple access methods including look ups using part numbers; looks ups using model numbers to find illustrations identifying part numbers and look ups using model or part descriptions; pricing, inventory and substitution data; illustrations which may be zoomed on the screen; optional 40 column pick-ticket/receipt printer; optional in-house or remote communications and an optional laser printer for illustrations.

A second example in the technical publishing area where CD-ROM systems are likely to complement and in some cases replace computer output microfiche systems is in the distribution of bibliographic databases or, more specifically, book ordering lists. We shall deal with some of these systems in more detail in the section on the library market but here we shall just take one example which shows how a CD-ROM system, while costing more than a microfiche based listing, can offer the user a host of additional valuable facilities.

Lasersearch is an electronic book identification and ordering system which is being offered by Ingram Book Company in the U.S. It makes use of the Library Corporation's ANY-BOOK bibliographic database on CD-ROM and the Lasersearch software was also developed for Ingram by the Library Corporation. The hardware comprises an IBM PC, XT, AT or compatible, a monitor and a Hitachi CD-ROM drive.

Using Lasersearch, an end user, bookseller or library staff member can search over one million English language book titles and access them via author, title, International Standard Book Number, LC number, publisher or keyword. The list includes the complete Ingram inventory and current publications list and all the titles which are available through Ingram are highlighted on the screen. Once the required title has been identified, orders can be transmitted directly from the user's computer to Ingram's computer via a telecommunications facility. The system has an electronic acquisitions management programme that can create, order and maintain up to 200 fund accounting records. The CD-ROM database is updated quarterly and excluding the computer, Ingram offer the system and the CD-ROM disc on a subscription basis at $795 a year. The disc on its own is $595.

Reference Technology, as well as being active in the in-house publishing field, are also active in technical publishing, having just signed an agreement with AMTEC Information Services of Lakewood, California. AMTEC recently introduced OPTI/Search, a laser optic publishing and information retrieval service that uses CD-ROM technology. AMTEC have the ability to merge text and art within a single database to allow rapid retrieval and display of textual information and associated artwork. Reference Technology will supply the laser optic system integration for AMTEC's product including disc preparation services, software and a variety of laser optic hardware products.

AMTEC has over 30 years experience in database management and publishing databases on various media. Examples include illustrated parts catalogues, shop and maintenance manuals, data sheets and data manuals for integrated component manufacturers and policy and procedure publications. OPTI/Search allows corporate clients to use microcomputer processing and CD-ROM storage to search, retrieve and display large volumes of publication information. Talking about the agreement with Reference Technology, Paul Kilker of AMTEC stated, "Our combined expertise in graphics integration, image conversion and enhancement, data services, application software and the ability to provide complete delivery system solutions provides valuable new CD-ROM capability. We will be able to service our clients better as they integrate paper and micrographics with CD-ROM technology".

There are already many more examples in the technical publishing field where CD-ROMs are being used to distribute information that used to be distributed on paper or on microfiche. In addition to being a more compact medium, the fact that CD-ROMs are an add-on computer memory means that by using CD-ROM the information is made more accessible and can be truly integrated into existing computer based systems. Today the cost of installing a CD-ROM based system is inevitably higher than a microfiche system but there is scope for significant price reductions over the next few years and when this is taken together with the numerous value-added features offered by CD-ROM systems, some of which have been outlined above, we feel confident that CD-ROM systems will have a very major impact in the in-house and technical publishing field, replacing paper and microfiche in some applications and themselves creating a number of new applications. We compare CD-ROM and microform systems in more detail in Chapter Six.

Other kinds of in-house and technical publications which will be distributed on CD-ROM in future but which we do not have the space to describe in detail here include: shipping schedules, budget plans, contracts, actuarial tables, mailing lists, meeting minutes, customer lists, annual reports, telephone books, operating instructions, product codes and descriptions, credit ratings, financial statistics, regulations, licensing agreements, medical information and emergency procedures.

5.3.3 Commercial publishing

As described above, commercial publishing is where a publisher identifies a market for a particular set of information, gathers the information or acquires the rights to it and then makes that information available to customers for a fee. The kind of information, the way in which it is distributed and the collection of end users who are prepared to pay for it will, of course, vary considerably. Here we are concerned with publishers who sell information to commercial and public sector organisations and we have divided the field up into six smaller categories, as follows: software distribution, graphic databases, database publishing, specialised information services, reference works and backfiles of serials.

5.3.3.1   Software distribution

Given that there is a large and ever growing base of computers in the world and that CD-ROM drives are a computer peripheral that can be attached to minicomputers and mainframes as well as microcomputers, it is obvious that one of the most attractive applications for CD-ROM will be as a software distribution medium. Indeed the computer companies are planning to use CD-ROMs to distribute not just operating system or application system software but also to distribute user documentation, manuals, tutorials and all the vast amounts of information that they need to support their computer users. Clearly any decision to use CD-ROM to distribute software would have considerable implications for a major computer supplier so we are unlikely to see any fast movement in this area but all the major computer companies are studying the potential cost savings that could be achieved and the potential benefits which could be offered to their customers.

Eric Coates of Digital Equipment Corporation gave a very clear indication of the potential of CD-ROM for software distribution at a talk he gave at the Optical Information Systems Conference run by Cimtech and Meckler Publishing in London in May 1986. The technical issues involved in connecting CD-ROM drives up to microcomputers, minicomputers and mainframes have all been solved by DEC. Indeed, since with software distribution it will be largely a question of downloading data from the CD-ROM onto a hard disk, problems such as the CD-ROM's slow access times can be avoided. In DEC's view CD-ROM technology is here and can be used to distribute a range of software including operating systems, executable programmes, data and documentation. The question is is it desirable, practical and economic for both the distributor and the user? DEC's work in this field has proved that CD-ROM systems are sufficiently reliable and will provide a low cost bulk distribution medium which costs as little as 2 pence per Mbyte in volume applications.

DEC currently has over 3,000 software products in its inventory and receives some 130,000 orders per year. It uses ten different media to distribute the software and documentation and has large automated warehouses to store, assemble and ship the software and documentation to customers. In many cases the documentation for a computer occupies more space than the computer itself. When virtually all of DEC's software could be fitted on one CD-ROM then the potential cost savings to DEC of using CD-ROM as an alternative to paper can begin to be appreciated.

However, there are problems to be overcome first. The first one is how DEC could ensure that the customer only got what he paid for? Coates felt secure that encryption would provide the answer here although there might be marketing problems as a user paid several thousand pounds and simply got an authorisation or password number sent in the post to him. The second problem is how DEC could administer the system. The difficulty would be in synchronising the release of different new software packages and revisions and in devising suitable access software to enable a range of users to access the manuals online.

None of these problems are insoluble and DEC are working hard, along with many other mainframe computer suppliers to develop a reliable mechanism for delivering their software on CD-ROM. When it happens, one would expect them to offer their customers very good deals on the CD-ROM hardware or even give them the hardware and recoup the money in consumable, postage, transport and staff savings. For the customers the benefits would include cheaper software, faster delivery and potentially, subsidised CD-ROM drives which could be used for other purposes.

This one application could result in a major installed base of CD-ROM drives being installed over the next two to three years as computer companies introduce the system to their major customers. Elsewhere, on a more modest scale, a number of other companies are offering software libraries on CD-ROM for PC users and this application is expected to grow. Again tutorial material, printed user manuals and documentation plus application and operating software updates can be distributed to users of popular microcomputers and personal computers and a number of companies are looking at CD-ROM as a way of distributing computer based audio training systems. Already in the U.S. Reference Technology have issued a CD-ROM disc containing a library of software for the IBM PC and Library Corporation has made available a CD-ROM disc containing PC user software. At the PC end of the market it is unlikely that CD-ROM will be ideal for distributing pure application software packages as most packages can be held on floppy diskettes but combined systems where several popular packages are stored on the disc together with all the documentation and an audio training programme could prove very attractive in future once the installed base of CD-ROM drives has built up.

5.3.3.2   Graphic databases

Here, bearing in mind the comments we made about the work that needs to be done relating to graphics on CD-ROMs, there are a wide range of attractive applications. Derek Painter of Cimtech gave a paper at the Cranfield conference held in July 1986 on the potential use of CD-ROM for distributing type font libraries to printers and publishers with their own desktop publishing systems. There are many thousands of different type faces available and each one needs to be raster scanned and stored in memory so that it can be called up and used at the laser printing stage when the user requests a particular type face. The amount of storage occupied by one high resolution raster scanned piece of type is considerable and only optical storage would allow large type font libraries to be offered in electronic publishing systems. Similarly, large in-house users or suppliers of electronic publishing systems could build up large libraries of scanned graphics - logos, scientific symbols, chemical structures, architectural symbols and computer flow chart symbols - and distribute those on CD-ROM for use in electronic publishing systems.

In addition, computer aided design users can expect libraries of standard graphics and symbols to be distributed to them on CD-ROM and there are CD-ROM applications in many more specialised computer systems with requirements for graphic data to be distributed to them for local processing. Graphic designers and printers could use a library of graphics distributed on CD-ROM which they could then pull off for use in creating their own designs or illustrating books and posters.

One very promising market will be for map information on CD-ROM. A map database on CD-ROM could be used for a wide range of applications including computer assisted navigational systems in planes, military vehicles and cars and for utility companies who could then overlay their services (e.g. pipes and telephone lines) and issue their service engineers with CD-ROM drives and monitors so they could locate broken water mains, etc. Philips have developed a computer assisted retrieval information and navigation system (CARIN) based around the use of CD-ROMs containing digitised maps which they expect to be made available in executive cars by the end of the decade (6). The main aim of the system is to reduce fuel consumption, decrease travel time and mileage and to monitor and link car functions and road and weather conditions. The system comprises a combined CD-ROM/CD audio player, on board microcomputer and monitor. On entering the car the driver enters his intended destination into the computer and then the road information on the CD-ROM is compared with the car's actual speed and route through dead reckoning. Route information is given to the driver through a speech synthesis unit which will also give instructions for correction if a deviation or wrong turn is made. Future refinememts of the system are expected to include the use of the European Radio Data system which broadcasts digital traffic information and can be used by CARIN so a route could be revised to take account of traffic jams.

Already, in the U.S., according to the U.S. CD Data Report Newsletter, a group of mappers, geographers and users of geographic data have met in Seattle and decided to form a special interest group to discuss technical issues not currently being addressed elsewhere. Called the CD-MAP forum, some of the issues which they intend to discuss are interactive mapping technology, data structures for mapping systems, standards and interchangeability and hardware.

5.3.3.3   Database publishing

While our first two categories of publishing may not be accepted as traditional commercial publishing applications by many in the publishing business, there can be little doubt that the third category - online database publishing - is a fully-fledged commercial publishing activity. It is also, not surprisingly, one of the first areas of the publishing community to take the potential of CD-ROM seriously. The leading conferences and exhibitions devoted to the online information industry, organised by Learned Information in the U.K. and U.S.A., have progressively increased the number of conference sessions and product review sessions devoted to the potential of CD-ROM publishing systems and the last year has seen a large number of exhibition stands showing prototype systems for distributing the whole or sub-sets of databases on CD-ROM. In addition, Learned Information and the various associations which represent the online information industry have, as described in Chapter Two, played a leading role in drawing up functional specifications for CD-ROM standards.

The online industry appeared to react to CD-ROM in one of four ways. There were those who, swept along with the tide of euphoria, saw CD-ROM as sweeping all other media aside and ushering in a new era of optical publishing. They rushed off and produced CD-ROM versions of their databases in order to take a piece of what they felt would be an enormous market. There were a considerable number who saw CD-ROM as offering them a new distribution medium which just as microfilm and online before it, would lead to an expansion of the market for their database products but would not significantly challenge existing media and they decided to experiment with prototype CD-ROM systems to analyse more fully the strengths and weaknesses of CD-ROM and assess the cost of producing a CD-ROM database.

There were those who saw CD-ROM as a potential threat to the online publishing market as it would divide the marketplace up, introduce another distribution channel which it would cost money to use but which, in the final analysis, would not lead to any major expansion of the market for online or electronic databases. In other words they felt it would fragment the market and they started to reexamine pricing policies for online products. Finally, a small percentage wrote off CD-ROM as a solution looking for a problem and one that was unlikely to have a major impact at all on the online publishing industry.

Taken together, the four reactions do summarise all the possible impacts which CD-ROM can have in the online database publishing market. CD-ROM can either be used as an alternative to an existing medium in an established application, e.g. publish a database on CD-ROM rather than make it available online, or it can be used alongside an existing system in an established application - publish a database on CD-ROM and make it available online as well and, in a best case scenario, significantly expand the market for the database, in a worst case, fragment the market and simply increase the overheads of the online database publishing industry - or use CD-ROM to create new applications combining sections of existing databases or distributing new databases or, finally, it may not be used at all.

The proponents of CD-ROM technology pointed to numerous advantages which CD-ROM had over online database distribution.

The key one was that currently the prohibitive cost of online services discourages many potential users from ever using an online database. With CD-ROM there was an opportunity to offer users a database on a yearly subscription basis and they would then be free to use it as much as they liked without incurring any additional costs.

Following on from this CD-ROM databases would represent an ideal way in which to teach online database users how to search a database.

Secondly, because CD-ROM would avoid the need to log-on and access databases via telecommunication links and CD-ROMs offered vast storage capabilities, they provided database providers and software suppliers with a golden opportunity to make the CD-ROM version of the database as easy to use as possible with numerous help facilities, multi-level search software so novices could use menus and experienced searchers could short circuit the system. In other words CD-ROM databases could be targeted at end users rather than skilled intermediaries such as librarians and information scientists.

Thirdly, there would be opportunities to package databases to meet the specific needs of identified users. In other words instead of one large legal database there could be numerous sub-sets of the legal database aimed at specific types of legal practice.

Inevitably, however, there were many database providers who did not want to wait and plan the most effective way of making databases available on CD-ROM, they simply wanted to produce a CD-ROM by placing sub-sets of their existing databases on CD-ROM. Not surprisingly, they were among the first companies, out of all the potential users of CD-ROMs described in this report, to show CD-ROM products. They had the databases already and, as we have seen in Chapter Three, many of the procedures involved in preparing a database for publication on CD-ROM and much of the retrieval software required emulated or was built upon what had been developed already for the online publishing industry. They were, therefore, in a better position than, for example, publishers of technical manuals and textbooks to place their databases on CD-ROM. However, a note of caution is due here as experience tends to indicate that the first applications identified for a new technology are not always, in the long term, the most successful ones. At the Online Conference in London in 1985 there were a whole host of database providers showing what they called CD-ROM versions of their database, although in effect, many of them were only small sub-sets of their databases.

Several CD-ROM system providers - most noticeably Digital Equipment Corporation and Silver Platter - put together complete data preparation, mastering, replication and retrieval hardware and software packages and signed a number of non exclusive agreements with the database providers to place all or sections of their databases on CD-ROM and market them, together with the necessary hardware and software, to the professional and library marketplace. However, as we have explained in previous chapters, these were somewhat premature systems as many of the necessary standards had not been agreed and little marketing research had been done to see what database users wanted or were prepared to pay, what price the database providers would have to charge to make a profit and what effect CD-ROM products would have on existing online revenues.

Predictably, therefore, despite the euphoria being created by consultants, CD-ROM suppliers and the press, the message began to trickle back from the users that while they found CD-ROM a fascinating technology with endless applications, they did not feel that simply placing a year of a database or in some cases, with very large databases, less than a year, on one CD-ROM was necessarily the best application for CD-ROM and they felt that the hardware was currently extremely expensive, they were worried by the apparent lack of standards, they did not feel that the software they were being offered was adequate to provide the sort of performance they had come to expect with online databases and they were finding that the prices being quoted for CD-ROM databases were far too high.

Similarly, the database providers have found themselves in a classic dilemma when it comes to pricing CD-ROM databases. On the one hand, in order to try and open up a wider market for their databases among end users and smaller companies, they need to keep the subscription price as low as possible. On the other hand, if they make their entire database available on CD-ROM at a relatively low cost they run the risk of losing a large part of their online income as heavy users of the online service decide to opt for the CD-ROM service instead.

A year later, some lessons have been learned and, not surprisingly, we have seen Digital Equipment Corporation announce that it has decided not to market actively databases on CD-ROM and instead is concentrating on data preparation services and providing its large corporate customers with in-house and technical publishing systems based around CD-ROM. Similarly, other online database providers have learnt by experience and are now taking a more realistic view of the potential of CD-ROM and, significantly, the host organisations such as Dialog and BRS are beginning to discuss their view of where CD-ROM fits into the online information business.

However, while the initial naive enthusiasm may have been dented, the picture is far from gloomy. We have seen several success stories and we still see an ever increasing number of information providers experimenting with CD-ROM and announcing prototype systems which, to an observer at least, appear to get closer and closer to what users will be prepared to pay for. What we will attempt to do here is point out some of the trends that appear to be emerging and highlight some of the key issues which will still need to be addressed before CD-ROM finds its real niche in what was formerly known as the online industry but which may have to be renamed the online/optical database industry.

a.   CD-ROM ideal where telecommunications services do not exist

One area where there clearly will be a market for selected existing online databases to be distributed on CD-ROM is in the third world and various remote locations where there are no suitable telecommunication links. For these users, many of whom have had to rely entirely on microfilm or printed bibliographies in the past, CD-ROM will offer their first opportunity to access large bibliographic databases via a computer system and the fact that the databases may be a month or six weeks out-of-date will not pose any significant problems.

The Commonwealth Agricultural Bureau (CAB), a major provider of agricultural databases to a worldwide audience, supports this thesis. Up until 1983 it relied on other hosts to market its online databases but it then began to maintain and supply its own databases using DEC VAX equipment and their online database now contains over two million abstracts. CAB have produced a prototype CD-ROM which is currently being assessed at forty sites worldwide, the majority in the third world. In most cases the CD-ROM drive and microcomputer have been supplied to the third world countries using grants from international research foundations. CAB are now committed to producing a second CD-ROM disc which will be their first production disc. CAB feel that CD-ROM has a number of advantages over online, microfilm and paper distribution systems but do not feel that it will replace any one medium.

Firstly, as pointed out above, they state that for many third world users CD-ROM is the only way of offering them interactive searching facilities as online is simply not possible. Secondly, they feel CD-ROM can play an important role in providing education/training in interactive searching as students can be left to experiment with the system without incurring high usage costs. Thirdly, they feel CD-ROM will enable them to subdivide and repackage their database, providing regional specific CD-ROMs, for example. Hence CAB are very enthusiastic about CD-ROM over the longer term.

It is churlish but nevertheless true to point out, however, that most publishers will not be able to rely on grants to achieve an installed base of CD-ROM players and microcomputers so the third world market will be very dependent on significant cost reductions in CD-ROM hardware.

b. Combined CD-ROM/online terminals required

Secondly, a number of database providers have shown terminals where users can use the same software to access databases online or locally via CD-ROM drives. It appears obvious now that in many applications, while it may prove economic and convenient to hold large static databases locally (i.e. previous years of an online database) there will still be a requirement to access the current database online to ensure that the most up-to-date information is accessed. H. W. Wilson have developed a PC based workstation which will offer access to databases online or on CD-ROM and will allow users to switch from one mode to another with one keystroke. The multi-purpose terminal is aimed at information specialists, library patrons and occasional users so Wilson have provided multi-level search software facilities. In the U.S. they have demonstrated their Wilsondisc system. The prototype CD-ROM disc holds seven of the 22 Wilsonline online databases, providing users of the terminal with local access to seven of their databases. Users wanting access to the other 15 databases or to the most current portion of the other seven databases can then go online to them. One feature of the Wilson terminal will be the facility for users to create a search in local mode (searching the CD-ROM), save it and then use the same search online.

Such combined terminals would certainly appear to offer database providers, hosts and users with the potential to develop and use hybrid systems which make best use of the two distribution alternatives.

Such terminals, when supplied by host organisations such as BRS and Dialog could also begin to solve the pricing dilemmas posed by CD-ROM. At the Online Conference in New York, Dr. Fred Zappert, Manager, Advanced Technology Group, Dialog Information Services Inc., gave an outline of Dialog's view of the future of CD-ROM in the online publishing arena. Dialog, as the world's largest online host, making databases available online, marketing those databases to end users, providing end users with retrieval terminals and search software and training users to effectively search the databases, is committed to provide increasingly effective means for accessing, presenting and disseminating recorded information through computer technology.

According to Zappert, this role does not limit Dialog to any particular technology such as online distribution. They see CD-ROM technology as part of this development and are optimistic regarding the application of CD-ROM to information retrieval. In examining the technology and discussing issues with several database producers they are finding opportunities and problems that have not been adequately addressed in early products and this has led them to formulate some product requirements.

"One problem is the proliferation of incompatible offerings from a number of companies. This Tower of Babel is confusing to potential customers.

In a formative market of technical products that are hard to compare and evaluate, customers look to a known source to present a market standard they can trust - in this case, to bring a critical mass of information together with uniform accessibility and quality, the way Dialog has done online.

DIALOG is the most widely used search system among information specialists, a group likely to be among the early adopters of CD-ROM products for information retrieval. We intend to include the same, familiar DIALOG features in the CD-ROM information products we distribute.

Another difficulty is the relative currency of CD-ROM products. In many cases, quarterly or even monthly updates delayed by the current turnaround time from CD duplicators cannot provide the currency expected by users. To provide the best of both media, we will provide integrated access where most searching can be done on disc and the latest updates are quickly available online.

CD-ROM also offer many opportunities for new pricing arrangements. The prospect of unlimited usage free of hourly charges is one of the most appealing aspects of CD-ROM products for information consumers and is, after all, the traditional way print publications are sold but information providers are justifiably concerned with the effects of various pricing schemes on their existing print and online products.

This concern over cannibalisation has caused some database producers to withold their most valuable information, yielding to CD-ROM only fragmentary information or information of less currency. We are working together with database producers to develop a solution to this problem acceptable both to them and to information consumers.

Finally, we expect to develop a complete product offering intended to assure the satisfaction of the information consumer. During our long experience with online distribution we have developed an extensive range of services that go beyond a search language and databases. We also offer training, complete documentation, customer support and regular customer communications and know that these services are critical for customer satisfaction. Our CD-ROM products will be supported with the same high quality services and will be integrated with our online offerings."

This outline of future directions would appear to confirm the view that combined online/CD-ROM access workstations will be offered by the major hosts and certain specialist database providers and that the existing online hosts could provide a solution to the problem of pricing. Online and CD-ROM subscriptions could be bundled together or, as one proponent of online services advocated, if CD-ROM databases are offered on a yearly subscription basis so will online databases. Alternatively, it may well prove possible to monitor the usage made of a CD-ROM database by one user and introduce a royalty billing system. In the U.S., according to a report in CD Data Report, a not-for-profit organisation called the Alexandria Institute, founded by Binx Shelby is designing a mechanism that will allow database providers or hosts to charge CD-ROM database users on a usage basis.

Hence we could see one time charges for access to online or CD-ROM databases or we could see usage charges for both online and CD-ROM access, whichever appears to make the most sense to the hosts, database providers and users.

Packaged database products may be most attractive to end users

The third point to emerge over the past year is that if CD-ROM is to open up new markets for online databases then the CD-ROM products will have to be aimed at end users rather than intermediaries such as information scientists and librarians. Two things follow from this realisation.

Firstly, the CD-ROM databases must be far more easy to use than current online databases. There must be adequate help facilities, simple menus, the use of user friendly front end systems and, as soon as possible, artificial intelligence must be used to help guide the user around the contents of the database.

Secondly, and more significantly, it will not be sufficient to simply make one year of an existing database available on one CD-ROM. Instead there will need to be co-operative agreements among database providers serving the same discipline - medicine, information technology, etc. - so that sub-sets from a number of databases can be published together on one CD-ROM with, ideally, common search software. These packaged database products would be targeted at the needs of particular professional and the most promising markets at present appear to be the financial, medical and scientific markets. In future such packaged products will be extended to include full text as well as bibliographic databases and we look at some of the early examples of these specialised information products below in the next section. One example of a packaged database product that has achieved a lot of publicity has been the Datext Corporate Information database.

The Datext Corporate Information Database (CID) combines information from several different data sources on CD-ROM. Their proprietary software then allows a user to search the databases, create a new file and transfer the blended information to other software programmes or spreadsheets for manipulation and analysis. Data from four information providers (Business Research Corporation, Disclosure, Media General and Predicasts) and from Datext themselves is organised by company and industry and stored on one of five CD-ROMs that represent broad industry sectors - consumer, industrial, services, technology and high technology. The discs are updated monthly. Aimed at the corporate end user in Fortune 1,000 companies the database now contains information on over 12,000 companies. The system allows comparison of corporate financial data over time. Finally, Datext has recently added an online option, providing a link to the Dow Jones News/Retrieval service to provide users of the corporate information database with current information and price quatations. As with the H. W. Wilson product, Datext have provided a software package which allows users to switch from CD-ROM to online and back again using an automatic log-on and log-off online service. The Datext workstation is based on an IBM PC XT or AT or compatible and as part of the subscription the user receives a Hitachi CD-ROM drive, a controller card and cable, maintenance, a software licence, documentation and one or more of the CD-ROM database products. Price for all the above and one CD-ROM database is $9,600 per year. The online option will be paid for in blocks of fifty or more hours.

Clearly the Datext system, with a monthly update service and key financial data is an expensive service and not typical in that sense. However, it illustrates well how CD-ROM will enable publisher to compile integrated systems targeted at specific user sectors and drawing on a number of different sources of information.

We list some of the many prototype CD-ROM systems which have been shown by online database providers to date in Chapter Nine. All we have been able to do here is comment on the trends that we have observed and point out some of what we see to be the most promising areas for CD-ROM based products. These are early days and only a very few companies have shown real commercial products. Over the next year we expect to see systems that follow the standards set by the High Sierra Group. We expect to see the hosts beginning to set up the necessary infrastructure and support services that will give users added confidence in combination online/CD-ROM distribution systems and we expect to see more an more packaged CD-ROM database systems targeted at end users.

5.3.3.4 Specialised information services

When we talk of specialised information services (SIS) here, we are referring to a relatively new form of publication which will receive a considerable boost with the advent of low cost reliable CD-ROM systems. Essentially SIS can be seen as an attempt to target specific groups of professionals, analyse their information requirements and produce specialised libraries comprising all the reference type information that these professionals need to carry out their work efficiently. It can be seen as a further development of the trend, identified in the previous section, towards packaged database products only here, in addition to bibliographic information, full text and even image data will be collected together as well.

There are a number of very successful examples of this type of publication in the microform publishing area. Barbour Index in the U.K. produce their Technical Microfile and Product Microfile, two microfiche collections which are aimed at architects, surveyors and other professionals in the construction industry. Information distributed on microfiche includes product catalogues, standards information and specialised reference works in the construction field. On a larger scale, Information Handling Services in the U.S. and Technical Indexes in the U.K. capture, microfilm, index and distribute vast collections of product catalogues, standards, technical specifications and regulations, divided up by subject or by a specific industry grouping and sell subscriptions to these specialised information products worldwide. Currently the material is just recorded in image form and access is provided via a hardcopy or online index.

In future these and other new publishers will begin to transfer firstly the index databases to CD-ROM and eventually, much of the full text information itself so that users will be able to search both the index and the full text information on CD-ROM via a low cost computer terminal. Two examples where CD-ROMs are now being used to distribute the indexes to full text stored on microfilm are provided by Newsbank and IHS.

Newsbank Inc. offer three services comprising full text articles on microfiche extracted from newspapers in some 300 U.S. cities. The 'Newsbank' service is composed of articles on current affairs and regional issues selected from these newspapers, 'Names in the News' provides full text newspaper articles on over 2,500 people annually and 'Review of the Arts' provides current newspaper reviews and articles on theatre, film, art and music. Their Newsbank Electronic Index contains five years of index information for these three services and it is now being offered on CD-ROM with a quarterly update option. The complete service comprising an IBM PC, HP printer, Hitachi CD-ROM player, software, a year's subscription to the index and updatings plus the microfiche service and hardcopy index for the current year is priced at $6,995 p.a.

IHS outlined their approach to CD-ROM in the March issue of their house magazine 'Info News'. They have carried out extensive surveys of users of their existing microform based services and have found that their customers continue to need the full text and graphics of specifications, standards, federal documents and catalogue data but that they now want it in an electronic form - retrievable and displayable on their own computer screens. Also needed is more detailed information in the indexes including parameters, part numbers and linkage to other databases.

With the development of CD-ROM, IHS will be able to place its enormous data files at an engineer's workstation and to make full use of this new delivery mechanism IHS is changing its internal data capture process to improve cross-referencing between databases as well as to ensure completeness and currency. In 1986, IHS in the U.S. will deliver its first CD-ROM service comprising information from selected VSMF indexes together with additional related data. Further, more ambitious projects are planned for 1987 but IHS are not considering discontinuing their microfilm products, rather they will simply be delivering their information in a wider variety of formats. At the AIIM show in May, which we attended, IHS were showing a prototype CD-ROM holding some 13,000 Comptroller General decisions and an index to all their equal opportunity commission decisions.

Some of the most promising application areas for SIS would appear to be the medical, legal, financial, scientific and technical areas where workers all need access to vast stores of recorded information. One interesting SIS in the medical arena is provided by a company called Micromedex. Their Computerised Clinical Information System (CCIS) is claimed to be the first medical information product available on CD-ROM which, according to an article by L. S. Rann (7) has been widely accepted by the medical community in a growing number of hospital and industry locations. Micromedex has authored and published medical databases and supplied them to over 1,500 pharmacies, emergency departments and poison control centres worldwide using microfiche and magnetic tape. The CCIS CD-ROM comprises four databases - Poisindex, Drugdex, Emergindex and Identidex - occupying in all some 300 Mbytes.

In the U.S., Prentice-Hall are developing what they call a tax resource library on CD-ROM which will be marketed to tax accountants. Called PHINET the library contains regulations, case studies, rulings and interpretations that together make up the critical body of U.S. tax law and occupy a total of 490 Mbytes. The PHINET CD-ROM has been prepared and mastered by Reference Technology using their retrieval software and is currently being evaluated in a number of text sites prior to being launched.

There are clearly many similar applications in the legal area. In the U.K. a consortium of British publishers, called Knowledge Warehouse, are establishing the first archive of books, journals and reference material held in electronic form. The venture will preserve electronic versions of books and exploit them commercially by reformatting them into electronic products. One of the ways of distributing the new products will be via CD-ROM and the first pilot project is to gather electronic versions of up to 200 works covering maritime commerce and law and produce a CD-ROM product from them to sell worldwide. The full text of the 200 maritime works will be held on the CD-ROM but the index will also be made available online. The project is being managed by Mandarin Communications, electronic publishing consultants.

In the areas of science and technology, as a first venture, a number of major publishers, including Pergamon, McGraw-Hill and Wiley are developing electronic versions of their specialised scientific and technical encyclopaedias which will be distributed on CD-ROM, making them simpler to use and of much greater value to scientists. Specifically, McGraw-Hill are planning to make available their twenty volume Encyclopaedia of Science and Technology on CD-ROM in 1987 together with a full index at a price, according to the U.S. CD Data Report, of $1,400.

There are numerous other applications which we could discuss further if we had space. It suffices to say that as the installed base of CD-ROM drives increases and as, due to the influence of standards and volume sales, costs drop, the number of SIS will increase and they will become increasingly more sophisticated and specialised until it becomes economically viable to produce SIS on CD-ROM that sell 100 or less copies, rather like today it is possible to produce vast microform collections and make a profit on sales of under 100.

5.3.3.5   Reference works

Clearly again the divisions merge and some specialised information services, particularly the encyclopaedias described above, could more reasonably be termed reference works - the dividing line depends on how specialised the reference work is and, crucially, on whether the material gathered together on one CD-ROM has been taken from a number of sources or simply taken from one existing source. In using the term reference works we had in mind those publishers who are currently developing CD-ROM versions of existing published directories, general encyclopaedias, dictionaries, telephone directories, travel guides and government statistics.

This area of the professional market overlaps with the library and consumer marketplace to an extent, just as today printed directories are sold into all three markets. The emphasis for the professional marketplace, however, will be on increasing the functionality of the directory by placing it on CD-ROM in coded form. As an example, with a printed directory of suppliers, a user has to scan through all the suppliers of a particular item, use various criteria to narrow the list, note down the names and addresses of the remaining suppliers and send off to them asking for further details or telephone them and ask for quotes. The same directory on CD-ROM could be accessed online, search criteria could be specified and modified and when the relevant supppliers had been identified standard letters could be generated with their names incorporated or orders could be generated automatically.

Many well known suppliers of directories are already experimenting with CD-ROM products including Dun & Bradstreet and the publishers of the Kompass directories. In addition, publishers of travel guides, telephone directories and many other utility type directories which are issued on a regular basis are evaluating the use of CD-ROM. Silver Platter have recently placed the Post Office's entire file of 23.5 million postcoded addresses onto a single CD-ROM which is selling for £2,500. The address file can now be used to find any private or business address in the U.K. within seconds. Previously the list was made available on microfiche and on magnetic tape for processing on mainframes. The magnetic tape version cost companies £12,000. The use of CD-ROM to publish a number of directories such as the Post Code list would, in addition, turn them into extremely valuable mailing lists where users could define a category of supplier or potential customer and then run a search and print out address labels from the.Directory.

In the Government sector clearly many economic statistics, census data, crime reports or consumer survey data could be made available at a premium on CD-ROM so that marketing departments and researchers could process the data and incorporate it into modelling systems.

5.3.3.6   Backfile/collection distribution

The above five applications, with the possible exception of some Specialised Information Services, relate primarily to the distribution of coded text, data and graphics on CD-ROM for users with PCs to search, process, manipulate and display or printout. In all cases the information distributed on CD-ROM would be actively used and processed by the end users and hence the CD-ROM product would have potentially considerably greater value than the equivalent printed product, if one exists. This last application area, with its rather awkward title refers to a specific area of publishing or republishing, largely dominated by the microform publishers which comprises the publishing of backfiles of journals and newspapers and the publication of collections of government reports, grey literature on microfilm.

Examples include the popular backfile copies of The Times distributed on 35mm microfilm and the U.S. Government reports distributed on microfiche by the National Technical Information Service (NTIS), the Educational Resource Information Centre (ERIC) and many others. Here microfilm is used as a cheap, compact way of distributing facsimile images of the pages of serials and reports which are usually purchased by company information centres to service requests for specific articles and reports. Typically the indexes to this material are available online so users can conduct a search, identify the specific articles they require and then request copies of those articles. To satisfy the request the library retrieves the microform, prints out the article or report using a reader-printer or copies the microform if it is a long report and sends the printout or the replicate microfilm to the user.

Such material can be held in-house by end users or they can use an external source of supply such as the British Library's Document Supply Centre. Such systems make economic sense as the index is actively used and hence is available online while specific articles or reports are used much less regularly so they are stored on a low cost medium - microfilm. However, in large information centres and in centralised document supply centres such as the British Library Document Supply Centre (BLDSC) where demand is high, the use of two or even three systems - online index databases plus full text on microfilm or, in many cases full text still on paper - is cumbersome and time-consuming to operate. Hence publishers (both publishers of the original material and microform publishers) and the document suppply centres are experimenting with new techniques for distributing images of articles and reports electronically either on CD-ROM or via facsimile networks.

At the Cranfield Conference held in July 1986, David Russon of the BLDSC spoke on future developments in this area. He reported a continuing growth in the demand for document delivery services from the BLDSC and described some of the new systems which they have either introduced or are planning to introduce in the near future to meet this demand. Firstly, they are offering electronic ordering facilities via the online database hosts so that once users have identified which articles they require as the result of an online search they can automatically order a copy of that article from the BLDSC. In addition the BLDSC are developing a customer workstation which large users of the BLDSC could use to access and search the BLDSC's stock list which will be distributed on CD-ROM. In addition to a CD-ROM drive and a PC, the terminal will include telecommunications facilities so users can obtain a status report to see whether the item is in stock at the BLDSC and place an order for it.

Secondly, the BLDSC are developing electronic facsimile delivery services. Currently they offer Group 3 facsimile but in future, as the public switched telephone network is replaced with a switched 64 Kbit network they could offer a much faster Group 4 facsimile service to customers prepared to pay a premium.

Thirdly, the BLDSC, together with the publishers consortium called ADONIS, are investigating the electronic storage and local delivery of facsimile images of selected journal articles held by the BLDSC. ADONIS are planning to place the contents of some 300 of the most popular journals in the biomedical field onto CD-ROM. The journal articles will be raster scanned using a CCD array scanner, digitised, compressed and stored on CD-ROM and ADONIS envisage issuing one CD-ROM per week. The CD-ROMs will replace the hardcopy of the journals at the BLDSC and at other document supply centres worldwide and will be used to satisfy requests for journal articles. When a request for an article on one of the 300 biomedical journals is received the relevant CD-ROM will be loaded into a drive and the article will be printed out on a high quality laser printer using a special CD-ROM image display and retrieval workstation which is currently under development. Eventually, if copyright and royalty arangements can be worked out then heavy users of these 300 core journals could be supplied with the CD-ROMs directly.

Hence heavy users of the BLDSC can expect over the next few years to be offered firstly bibliographic databases on CD-ROM and electronic ordering facilities, then the option of having full text material delivered to them directly via high speed facsimile networks and finally, as an option, to have the full text of specific core journals delivered to them at regular intervals on CD-ROM.

A similar system has been demonstrated by one of the largest microform publishers in the world - University Microfilms International - who were recently acquired by Bell & Howell. UMI, in conjunction with TMS, a CD-ROM system provider, produced a prototype combined bibliographic and image database on CD-ROM in the U.S. which was demonstrated to us in the U.K. by Archetype who offer the TMS system in the U.K. UMI are looking to supply an add-on subsystem to the growing number of PC based library automation systems, which they call their Information Delivery Module. The base workstation is the OCLC M300 or an IBM PC and the UMI module comprises two distinct elements. The first is for receiving and printing digitally transmitted images - the facsimile option described above in our account of work at the BLDSC and the second element is for retrieving, displaying and printing document images and data stored on either CD-ROM or hybrid videodiscs. To demonstrate the system UMI had placed a section of the INSPEC bibliographic database on CD-ROM together with facsimile images of all the articles indexed in a year. The retrieval workstation allowed a portion of each article page to be displayed at full resolution or the entire page to be displayed at reduced resolution and hardcopy was provided via a laser printer operating at 200 dots per inch.

As we said above, there are several technical problems to be overcome before large collections of images can be distributed commercially on CD-ROM but it appears that the publishers and the document supply centres see sufficient advantages in such systems to invest considerable amounts in thei development. One key factor, of course, will be the fact that publishers will be able to monitor the usage made of articles via document supply centres and charge a royalty.

In looking at potential commercial publishing applications for CD-ROM any attempt to divide the field up can be challenged on a number of grounds. All we have tried to do is give a flavour of the enormous range of potential applications where CD-ROM appears to offer benefits over any of the existing alternatives in the hope that it may set some publishers thinking and innovative new products will result.

We feel that for the short to medium term at least professional applications will constitute by far the largest market for CD-ROM systems because these are the applications where productivity gains can be easily measured and paid for and where the necessary base of computer expertise lies. There are many promising applications in the library and educational sectors but these will inevitably play second fiddle to the professional marketplace. The consumer marketplace, while potentially huge and hence very attractive to publishers, is still the most uncertain of the markets for CD-ROM or CD-I systems and we can only hazard a guess as to some of the applications that may take off there and the likely timescale over which CD-ROM and CD-I systems will be introduced and accepted into the home.

5.4   The library market

As described above, we decided to deal with the library market for CD-ROM publications separately, not because we expect it to be a particularly large market but because it was one of the first potential market areas to be targeted and there are already a number of CD-ROM products aimed at the libraries.

At the outset one can divide the library market into two distinct categories. The first we shall call the library automation market and it relates to the use of CD-ROM based systems in order to automate existing library procedures or to further enhance existing library automation systems. Examples here can be found in the cataloguing area and the acquisitions area - two crucial aspects of any library automation system and ones where CD-ROM can play a significant role.

The second area is the more traditional one which relates to the potential purchase of CD-ROM publications by libraries as part of their stock. Today libraries buy books, subscribe to journals, buy microfilm collections and subscribe to online database services. In the future will they purchase CD-ROM publications or subscribe to CD-ROM based services and, if so, which ones?

In addition to these two categories there will, of course, be large national libraries or specialist libraries who will themselves become publishers of information on CD-ROM - distributing portions of their collections on CD-ROM - and others who will investigate the potential of CD-ROM as an archiving medium but here we are concentrating on libraries as a potential market for CD-ROM publications and services.

5.4.1 Library automation systems

One of the first and most obvious applications for CD-ROM systems in the library market was the distribution of bibliographic databases. There are numerous such systems, some of which are designed specifically for current and retrospective cataloguing purposes, some of which are part of automated book ordering systems and some of which are primarily for reference purposes.

The Library Corporation in the U.S. have produced a catalogue production system which they call their 'Bibliofile' which is based around a CD-ROM subsystem connected to an IBM PC. Some 1.4 million MARC records are stored on two CD-ROMs, containing all the Library of Congress's English language catalogue entries since 1964 plus popular titles since 1900 and libraries can use the system for retrospective catalogue conversion, the creation of MARC tapes and the printing of catalogue cards and labels. The software provides access to the MARC database and users can download records, edit them and add new records prior to printing them out.

In the U.K., Sydney Library Systems, suppliers of an IBM PC library automation system have incorporated the Bibliofile CD-ROM subsystem into their system and can now provide users of their Micro Library system with instant access to the entire LC MARC database. They offer a quarterly or monthly update service for the CD-ROMs and will provide the CD-ROM hardware in the U.K., the interface board for the PC and all software. The complete system including CD-ROM drive, software and the database on CD-ROM costs £2,500.

Following the success of the Library Corporation's system in the U.S., OCLC, the giant U.S. provider of bibliographic services to libraries, have shown their own CD-ROM based cataloguing and reference systems. OCLC's Compact Disc Cataloguing System uses a subset of the OCLC Online Union Catalogue stored on a CD-ROM disc. The package will support local cataloguing and card production using a MARC database distributed on CD-ROM. It will also communicate with the Online System to search for additional records, add or update records and produce catalogue cards, labels and MARC records. Approximately 500,000 bibliographic records and their indexes will be distributed on each CD-ROM and OCLC is apparently considering producing subsets of records in several categories. Databases will be offered on a subscription basis with monthly or quarterly cumulative updates. The system will run on an OCLC M300 workstation with 640K RAM, a 20 Mbyte hard disk card and a CD-ROM drive. Other companies who have shown similar CD-ROM based cataloguing subsystems include Horizon, UTLAS and Carrolton.

Moving onto automated book ordering systems, Ingram Book Co. were one of the first to show a CD-ROM based system which they call their Retail Lasersearch system. Aimed primarily at bookstores, the concept is equally applicable to libraries. The hardware comprises a CD-ROM drive linked to an IBM PC and the database comprises the Library Corporation's Any Book database of some 1.5 million English language titles. Using the software provided users can identify any book by author, title, subject or publisher and those titles available ex stock from Ingram Book Company are highlighted. Orders can be placed electronically to Ingram or printed orders can be produced for other suppliers. The system offers flexible fund accounting with the capability to maintain up to 200 fund accounts. The subscription price of $795 p.a. covers rental of a CD-ROM drive, applications software plus quarterly updates of the CD-ROM database.

There are many more bibliographic databases being prepared which could be used for reference or ordering purposes depending on where they are installed. R. R. Bowker have shown a CD-ROM version of their Books in Print which they are calling BIP Plus. One CD-ROM holds all five BIP publications and the software package offers sophisticated searching, browsing and formatting facilities. Once selected the records can be printed on catalogue cards or on order forms etc. Indeed, there is a facility to permit users to send orders electronically to Ingram and other US book suppliers. BIP is expected to be available in late 1986 at a price of $895 including quarterly updates. In the U.K. Whitakers, in co-operation with the British Library, produced a prototype CD-ROM with records from their British Books in Print database and the British Library's BLAISE database on it. Whitakers are understood to be investigating the market for a CD-ROM version of their British Books in Print which could be offered with an automated book ordering facility to booksellers and librarians.

From the provision of cataloguing and acquisitions systems based around CD-ROM it is a short step to the provision of CD-ROM based document delivery systems of the type shown by University Microfilms International and described by the British Library and the ADONIS consortium, which we described in the previous section.

Other areas where CD-ROM systems could be employed in future library automation systems include the distribution of a public or academic library's catalogue - the so called optical catalogue described by Joseph Cavanagh of the State University of New York(8) - and the storage of library shelf lists/client lists.

5.4.2 Databases and reference material on CD-ROM

In order to talk meaningfully about the potential library market for CD-ROM databases and reference publications, we must first define exactly what we mean by libraries. Traditionally there are three categories of library - public, academic and special - and they all have different roles to play and different purchasing patterns.

By special we are referring to company libraries and information centres, libraries in public sector organisations including government departments, libraries in research establishments and professional associations and practices and finally, large national libraries. Initially, we feel that special libraries are likely to represent the most lucrative market for CD-ROM databases just as they are the heaviest users of online databases. These will be followed by academic libraries and finally by public libraries. There are a number of key issues which will determine librarians' attitudes to CD-ROM based products.

The first one is the question of standards. They will not want to have to install different hardware to access different databases on CD-ROM, they will want to standardise on one PC, one interface and one CD-ROM drive for ease of servicing. They will expect to be able to access any CD-ROM databases using that hardware configuration.

The second one relates to the logistics and security issues raised by CD-ROM. When microfilm was first introduced into libraries as a stock item librarians were unsure how to handle it, where to site readers and reader-printers, whether to put the microfilm on open access or lock it away for security, who would be responsible for the maintenance of the film and the hardware. Over the years the problems were gradually overcome through the use of microfilm areas and dedicated microfilm librarians but not before many users were deterred from using microfilm because of poorly sited or poorly maintained equipment.

Similarly when online systems were introduced there were problems due to the cost of using the systems online and the need for trained operators which restricted the use of online systems by end users. It appears as if CD-ROM systems will usher in a new set of logistical problems which, unless solutions can be found quickly and efficiently, will restrict the usage made of them in libraries. In public and academic libraries there will be a security problem and users will have to request CD-ROM databases, sign for them and return and have them checked out. In addition there is the question of whether the CD-ROM databases and the search software will be simple enough for end users to use themselves or whether a shortage of PCs in the library will result in restricted usage and staff being required to conduct searches for users. In addition, with popular databases there will be the problem of contention which may be met by introducing multi-user CD-ROM systems of the type being developed by Silver Platter or by simply ordering two copies of the disc. An added problem will be the provision of printout services and how they will be charged for.

The third one relates to the type of material which will be required by the various library markets. Clearly many of the special libraries will have specialist interests mirroring the interests of the professional association or research body or company that they are designed to serve. Such libraries typically regularly use some two or three core databases online and a number of others on an infrequent, as needs, basis. To such libraries it might prove attractive to purchase all or sub-sets of the core databases on CD-ROM in future and use them on combined online/CD-ROM terminals so that, if required, they can also go online to other databases or to check the latest version of the core databases.

In the academic field the emphasis might be more on reference type material on CD-ROM including some of the directories, technical encyclopedias and dictionaries which are being placed on CD-ROM and in the large reference departments of public libraries there would be a similar demand for such products.

In a report (9) we wrote recently for IFLA (the International Federation of Library Associations) we summarised the position as follows:

'Most librarians we have spoken to will be looking for two things from optical publishing. Firstly, valuable material becomes cheaper and/or easier to access on optical disc than on paper, microfilm or online or is only available on optical disc. Secondly, some degree of standardisation emerges both in the hardware, the media and the organisation of the data so that optical discs purchased from a range of publishers/information providers can be read in a range of disc players from different suppliers, attached to a range of microcomputers from different suppliers. When these two preconditions are met then libraries will invest in the necessary optical disc hardware.'

As we have shown in Chapters Two and Three, standard hardware and software should be available within the next 12 months and we would expect special librarians to begin seriously purchasing stock items on CD-ROM within the next 18 months to two years. The type of reference and database material which libraries purchase on CD-ROM has already been described in the previous section on the professional market. A brief list of products announced to date appears in Chapter Nine. Those requiring a more detailed consideration of some of the library applications for optical disc systems are referred to the IFLA report (9).

Before leaving this section we must also point out that if many of the predictions being made about the imapct of optical publishing over the next five to ten years prove valid then the role of special libraries in particular is set to diminish quite considerably over the next ten years anyway. As we have shown when looking at the professional market, the aim of the publishers is to move away from selling databases to intermediaries and instead to make them specialised enough and easy enough to use so they can be marketed to the end users direct. Instead of going to a secretary or a librarian to find old cuttings in a newspaper or to compare figures of a group of companies the end user will be able to access the cuttings and the figures directly via a PC and a set of CD-ROMs containing specially tailored databases designed to cater for his specific requirements. This is the theory and in certain applications such as the financial and legal areas and certain of the engineering disciplines where data is structured and requests can be easily formulated we can already see that the trend towards individual knowledge support systems is irreversible. In the bulk of cases, however, where a number of end users need access to the same databases and where the databases are complex and terms and search strategies change, it would appear likely to remain far more cost effective for one specialist to be in charge of using the databases - whether online or on CD-ROM - than a group of highly paid knowledge workers who will differ in their desire and ability to conduct their own searches.

We could write an entire report on the impact of CD-ROM and optical publishing systems on the role of library and information centres. Suffice it to say that while we feel it represents a move away from centralised information services to the local provision of information resources we feel it is only a small move and one which will be resisted in some quarters and could take many years to prove significant.

5.5   The educational market

The term education covers a wide area of applications where CD-ROM publications could be used. The first area, of course, is in the administrative side of education where the requirements will be similar to those in any of the professional markets described above. Following this there are applications in the primary and junior schools, secondary schools, further and higher education and the general market for educational and training products.

Applications for CD-ROM publications in the administrative area will include catalogues of audio visual aids and educational products for distribution to education authorities, distribution of educational databases such as the ERIC (Educational Resources Information Centre) database on CD-ROM and distribution of prospectuses, short course information and educational statistics on CD-ROM. Already in the U.K., ECCTIS (the Educational Counselling and Credit Transfer Information Service) are considering offering a version of their online database of courses at U.K. polytechnics and universities on CD-ROM together with related databases such as a careers information database and have already produced a prototype CD-ROM databse in-house. They envisage eventually offering volatile data such as their vacancy list online so it can be updated every night and then offering courses data and careers information on CD-ROM with a six monthly or quarterly update service. Much of the early development work for this project has been done in-house at the Open University's academic computing centre in Milton Keynes. In the U.S., according to the excellent CD Data Report several companies have announced CD-ROM products targeted at the educational establishment.

Tescor Inc. have announced a CD-ROM system called the National Item Bank and Test Development System which aims to enable teachers and educational administrators to create individualised tests, print them out and score and analyse the results. The CD-ROM comprises 40,000 test questions that have been used and validated by teachers in the past. In use a teacher would specify a particular test and the level of the pupils and the Tescor software would search the disc and select the test items that match the request. The teacher can then choose from the list of retrieved items the specific material to be used in a specific test and they are printed out. Tescor plans to update the disc with new questions twice a year and offers a wide range of workstation options priced at $4,500 per year and upwards.

A second company, Quantum Access Inc., based in Houston, Texas, are developing a CD-ROM database product that will contain all the legislative and regulatory material that a Texas school administrator is likely to need - including state legislation, policies and procedures of the Texas Education Agency, curriculum guides, transcripts of administrative hearings and court cases. The education regulations disc will be sold as a subscription service and Quantum plan to follow it up with a disc containing all the federal regulations required by school administrators.

Many of these products are strictly prototype and the economics may not make much sense in the U.K. but they do provide an insight into the sort of material that can be distributed on CD-ROM, once production and hardware costs decline, and the way in which CD-ROM products can be tailored to meet the needs of very specialised groups of end users.

Moving onto the schools, colleges and universities themselves, there are clearly many applications for CD-ROM and eventually CD-I based systems but there are equally obviously a number of major barriers to widespread acceptance of CD-ROM and CD-I products.

In primary and junior schools in particular there is a chronic lack of resources and advocates of CD-ROM and CD-I products will be in competition with educationalists seeking money for established media including textbooks, VCR's, scientific equipment and, increasingly, interactive videodisc systems of which a number have recently been developed for the schools sector. Indeed, we may learn much about the potential for CD-ROM and, in particular CD-I, in education by reviewing the painfully slow progress which interactive videodisc systems have made in the educational sector.

A number of companies in the U.K. and U.S. have now launched interactive videodisc systems aimed at the schools marketplace and the Department of Trade & Industry, through the National Interactive Video Centre (NIVC), is sponsoring and supervising the development of interactive videodisc courseware aimed at all levels of education but progress has been slow for a number of reasons. Firstly, when videodisc systems were first introduced there was a paucity of authoring systems and production tools of all kinds. Secondly, it took time for companies to gain the necessary expertise and build up the skilled teams needed to ensure that videodisc courseware was produced on time and in budget. Thirdly, the cost of videodisc courseware production proved to be so high that producers adopted a wait and see approach and only undertook commissioned work. Fourthly, a key factor was the lack of standardisation in interactive videodisc systems which meant that producers of courseware had to specify which computer or which videodisc player the courseware had been designed for and meant that all the early videodisc systems were sold into closed user networks - the military, car manufacturers, the chemical industry - and no-one attempted to open up a generic videodisc publishing market like the schools market. Fifthly, due to the sheer cost of the hardware and, as we have said, the lack of resources in the educational sector.

A classic example of the problems facing publishers of optical disc based products in the education sector is the BBC's Domesday Project. The concept - to conduct a census of Great Britain in the 1980s - was a good one and the material comprising local data collected by schoolchildren, photographic material, maps and statistical data supplied from government and commercial sources is undoubtedly of great value but the choice of a totally new piece of hardware (Philips' Laservision ROM a hybrid videodisc system that can store both analogue and digital data) has meant that the original intention - making a copy of the discs available to all the schools in the U.K. who participated in the project so that they could access the material via their BBC microcomputers - is now little more than a pipedream unless the DES or DTI provide the money. In addition to the Laservision ROM player, the schools will have to purchase a second dedicated microcomputer as their existing early BBC microcomputers are simply not powerful enough to control the system.

As described in earlier chapters, CD-ROM and, more particularly, CD-I will overcome many of the problems which hit the interactive videodisc industry - namely which computer and which player to link up and what other material could be read on one specific interactive videodisc system. In the case of CD-I the aim is to ensure that text, data, graphics and audio can be recorded on a CD-I and played back via any CD-I player. In the case of CD-ROM, once the High Sierra Group standard has been adopted and Microsoft launches the extensions to their MS-DOS operating system, it should prove possible to connect CD-ROM drives to all the IBM PCs and compatibles on the market and interfaces are also being developed between CD-ROM drives and the Apple microcomputer range.

Assuming that technical problems are overcome and costs decrease to the stage where CD-ROM drives and PCs are available for £500-600 or CD-I players sell for a similar amount, what are the main applications, bearing in mind the limitation that CD-I and CD-ROM do not offer high quality moving video?

In primary and junior schools there is still the logistical problem that CD-ROM and CD-I based programmes will be largely for individual instruction with a high degree of interactivity and hence not ideally suited to classroom teaching. The sort of courseware that could prove attractive would include educational games where responses from the class or a small group would lead to visual responses on the screen and, as an audio visual aid, slide sequences with audio commentary and questions and answers which again led to different slides being shown and different audio commentary.

In the secondary school there will be more scope for individualised instruction or programmes geared to small groups and we would expect to see systems installed in libraries, audio-visual laboratories and in computing departments. One key application area, described above, will be the distribution of software, documentation and tutorial packages to school computer departments to both help train students in the use of computer systems and to use the storage potential of CD-ROMs to help enhance existing computer based training systems. Educational games and modelling systems look attractive in this area while, in the library environment, encyclopaedias and phonetic dictionaries, of the type demonstrated by Grolier, Microsoft and Philips could prove attractive.

The educational market may well depend to a large extent on the degree of acceptance which CD-ROM and CD-I products find in the consumer marketplace. With the low cost of PCs we may well reach the stage where pupils can receive tuition at school based around a CD-ROM or CD-I product and then go home and use the same product to help them with homework.

In the higher educational sector the potential for CD-ROM and CD-I products is still more promising, particularly in areas where training courses are particularly expensive and involve the use of expensive hardware and consumables, e.g. medicine, chemistry, biology, botany, electronic and mechanical engineering. In these environments it will prove cost-effective to use simulated systems and the students are motivated to use self-instructional learning materials. Clearly the visual content in many training programmes is crucial so we may see combination CD-ROM and videodisc systems used in this application or the hybrid videodisc systems described above.

Also in higher education, trainee lawyers, accountants, doctors and engineers will increasingly have their own PCs in the home and coursework, textbooks and specialised libraries will be made available on CD-ROM so that they can study at home without the need to visit libraries and be tied by their opening hours. A related area where CD-ROM offers considerable potential is in computer controlled audio training systems where responses keyed in by the student result in different tracks of audio being played. Such systems would be ideal for language learning and many other self instructional applications.

Finally, we move outside of the formal educational environment and look at the market for training and self-instructional systems as a whole, whether provided by companies for in-service training or as part of Open University courses or simply for self-advancement. Again CD-ROM based audio training packages could be offered at a relatively low cost and specialised CD-ROM libraries containing all the background material you need to pass a particular examination together with past papers and question and answer sessions would find a ready market.

The potential is limitless but exeeperience gained with interactive videodisc systems shows that production of good courseware requires considerable skills and major investment and publishers will need to be confident that the market exists before they invest in such systems. Where CD-ROM systems could score over videodisc systems at this stage is that, provided the content is restricted to text, data and audio material, production costs could be considerably lower and the hardware costs will be lower too as the price of PCs continues to fall and once half height CD-ROM drives become available in volume. Where high quality moving video is required then interactive videodisc will still be preferred until, as Philips are now promising, CD-Video Interactive systems are launched where the CD spins at higher speed and short extracts of full motion video can be provided.

In identifying potential applications for CD-ROM/CD-I in education, we have not attempted to predict whether CD-ROM or CD-I systems will be selected. This is largely because, as described in Chapter One, very little is still known about CD-I and we would want to see prototype CD-I players and early CD-I products before trying to make more detailed predictions about the likely market split between CD-ROM and CD-I in education. One point that we would emphasise, however, is that courseware making use of all the facilities offered by CD-I - mixed data, text, audio and still and moving graphics, will be very expensive to produce and will only be produced when companies are convinced that a mass marketplace exists for it. Prototype CD-I players are not due until late 1987 and prototype products are therefore unlikely to follow until 1988. In addition 8mm video and digital audio tape systems will be available by then and competing with CD, CD-ROM and CD-I for a share of the domestic consumer and educational marketplace. We therefore, do not expect major commercial CD-I products to be launched until 1988/89 and would view with caution any suggestion that CD-I will significantly impact the educational market in the U.K. and Europe before 1990.

5.6   The domestic consumer market

Because of its enormous size and hence the potentially enormous rewards that greet the producer of any new product that captures a large share of it, the domestic marketplace has always fascinated suppliers and there is a ready store of examples where products have been targeted at the domestic consumer market, failed to make an impact and subsequently found a niche in a far more specialised marketplace serving the needs of business. One of the most recent examples was the videodisc, the technology which, as described in Chapter One, went on to spawn the entire range of compact discs and digital optical disks. The lack of a record facility meant videodiscs could never compete with video cassette recorders in the domestic marketplace and there are many who predict that the lack of a record facility on CDs, CD-ROMs and CD-I will make them vulnerable to a digital recording medium - namely digital audio tape (DAT) systems in the domestic market in future.

To date Compact Disc players have proved very successful. In the past three years since their launch, some 5 million players have been sold worldwide. To put this in perspective, however, this still represents just one sixtieth of the estimated 300 million record players currently installed in the world and an even smaller percentage of the number of audio cassette recorder/players in the world today. In the U.K. CD players are said to have achieved a 4% penetration of the marketplace, 1% short of the 5% needed for a product to be regarded as established.

Within the next six months domestic consumers are likely to be confused by the launch of yet another consumer high quality digital audio system - DAT. DAT systems represent the next generation of audio cassette systems and employ the same digital recording techniques as CDs. The sound quality obtained from DATs is equal to that of CDs, DATs can be copied without any degradation, the cassettes are half the size of existing audio cassettes so portable and in-car recorder/players can be produced and, like CDs they play on one side only and offer 2-3 hours of playback compared to one hour on a CD and 45 minutes on an audio cassette. Other facilities offered by R-DAT (a digital audio tape system with a rotating record/read head closely related to the heads used in VCRs) include the use of digital markers so individual tracks can be retrieved automatically, the ability to rewind a complete tape in 10-15 seconds and compatibility - the R-DAT standard has been agreed by some 150 companies worldwide. The only drawbacks at present are the recorder price - £1,000 per recorder and likely to remain at least 50% higher than CD players and the price of cassettes - currently estimated at £22 compared to £10 for a CD.

While consumers are being deluged with CD and DAT systems alongside LP and audio cassette systems on the audio front there will also be a battle waging in the video area between existing VCRs and 8mm systems and a whole new range of digital and cable television systems. Finally, there will be ever more powerful and lower cost PC systems offered to the domestic consumer. Against this background one has to look at what the consumer's priorities are going to be and what percentage of his income he is going to be prepared to spend on entertainment and educational systems.

As pointed out in the sections on the professional and domestic markets, there will be a growing trend for students and executives to take work home and use a PC at home to do that work. In many cases that will involve them in using databases, reference works and spacialised information products on CD-ROM. In addition, domestic PC users will want to use the sophisticated games that they will be offered on CD-ROM and CD-I. The extra storage capacity offered by CDs will enable games designers to produce high quality graphics, stereo sound and animated sequences which will bolster flagging demand for games products. Despite the considerable sums that will need to be invested in producing such games and the high cost of initial products, computer ganes companies in the U.S. and U.K. are all expressing considerable interest in CD games and see it as the inevitable way forward for computer games.

Another area pointed to by Philips was high quality audio plus pictures of pop stars and text describing their background. This application seems far less attractive as VCR systems with stereo audio could do the job equally well and the cost of purchasing combined CDs would be high.

The self-instructional area is a promising one with low cost audio based training systems and more expensive encyclopaedias and phonetic dictionaries looking attractive. Again ,however, there are numerous technical and economic issues to be addressed here. The cost of producing a multimedia encyclopaedia of the type shown in prototype form by Microsoft would be many millions of pounds. In addition it would occupy many CD-ROMs as the moving graphics occupy several Mbytes of storage each and encyclopedias comprise many thousand such graphics.

To date the only encyclopaedia available on CD-ROM is the Grolier Academic American Encyclopaedia and the version currently available is restricted to textual information only. Knowledgeset, a CD data preparation company set up by Gary Kildall, have worked with Grolier to place the entire text of the 21 volume encyclopedia on CD-ROM. Their Knowledge Retrieval System running on an IBM PC or Atari 520ST can provide the full-text search and retrieval facilities, providing instant access to every occurrence of a word, topic, group of words or phrase in the entire encyclopaedia in an average search time of 5-15 seconds. The CD-ROM version of the Academic Encyclopaedia together with the software is currently being offered at the low price of $199 or a complete package including a CD-ROM drive and interface is priced at $995.

Clearly Knowledgeset and Grolier would have to sell many thousands of copies of the CD-ROM encyclopedia to make a return on their considerable investment but they have demonstrated that such a largescale electronic publishing project can be achieved and when there is a larger base of installed CD-ROM or CD-I drives then major products such as the Academic American Encyclopaedia could be provided, with many value added features at prices considerably below the price of the equivalent printed version.

Intuitively, we feel less confident that there is a market for CD-ROM and CD-I products in the home than we do concerning the very many obvious applications for CD-ROM publications in the professional marketplace. Indeed the most promising markets we see for CD-ROM in the home largely ape the professional applications and hence will be largely restricted to students and professional people.

The market for CD-ROM or CD-I based encyclopaedias, dictionaries and reference works is never likely to equal that for the equivalent printed products and will take a long time to develop and prove costly for many publishers.

The final consumer market - for high quality games and combined audio/visual presentations - is one where CD-I and CD-ROM will have to compete with other inherently cheaper and more versatile products such as 8mm video, cable and satellite television and Digital Audio Tape systems. Until we see CD-I players and prototype CD-I products we would not like to comment on CD-I's chances in this cut-throat marketplace.

REFERENCES

1.   CD-ROM market opportunities study. Link Resources and Infotech. £3,500. Link Resources Corporation, 2 Bath Road, London.

2.   OM-20 CD-ROM and OROM products, applications and markets. $995. Optical Memory News, 256 Laguna Honda Boulevard, San Francisco, CA 94146-1496, U.S.A.

3.   PC optical disk market in the U.S.A. Report A 1636, $1900. Frost & Sullivan, Sullivan House, 4 Grosvenor Gardens, London SW1W 0PH.

4.   Market reports on CD-ROM and scanning systems. Diversified Data Resources Inc., 6609 Rosecroft Place, Falls Church, VA 22043, U.S.A.

5. RUDNICKY, P. Private information distribution: a Digital Equipment Corporation Study, pp 172-176 in 1985 Videodisc, Optical Disk and CD-ROM Conference and Exposition. Conference Proceedings, Meckler Publishing, 11 Ferry Lane West, Westport, CT 06880, U.S.A.

6. ROYCE, I. CARIN: an application of CD-ROM. Optical Information Systems, Vol. 6, No. 1., pp 53-59, Jan/Feb 1986, Meckler Publishing.

7. RANN, L. S. Optical disc applications in niche markets, pp 161-164 in 1985 Videodisc, Optical Disk and CD-ROM Conference and Exposition. Conference Proceedings, Meckler Publishing, 11 Ferry Lane West, Westport, CT 06880, U.S.A.

8. CAVANAGH, J. M. A. A proposed distributed pptical catalogue: a new basis for library automation, pp 36-42 in 1985 Videodisc, Optical Disk and CD-ROM Conference and Exposition. Conference Proceedings, Meckler Publishing, 11 Ferry Lane West, Westport, CT 06880, U.S.A.

9. HENDLEY, A. M. Optical disk systems: a guide to the technology and the applications in the fields of publishing and library and information work. IFLA Report No. 12. May 1986. ISBN 9070916 150. 60pp.

6. COMPARISON WITH TRADITIONAL PUBLISHING MEDIA AND SYSTEMS

6.1 Introduction

In the previous chapter we looked at the potential of CD-ROM systems in a range of specific application areas. In this chapter, because it is simply not possible to cover all the possible application areas where CD-ROM could be used or where it needs to be considered and compared with paper, microfilm and online alternatives, we want to set up some general rules or guidelines which will help commercial or in-house publishers to compare the various media - some rules of thumb which illustrate graphically the true benefits and limitations of the different media. The simplest way to do this is to set all the four alternative distribution media - CD-ROM, paper, microfilm and online electronic distribution systems - against a standard set of criteria.

The main criteria which need to be considered in any general comparison of publishing/distribution media include:

> Storage capacity
> Type of material - graphics/colour/moving video/resolution quality
> Ease of production
> Cost of production/replication
> Cost/ease of distribution
> Turnaround times
> Ease of updating
> Retrieval hardware required
> Portability of medium
> Accessibility of information
> Ease of use and user acceptance
> Ease of integration with existing systems

Using these criteria we will attempt to gauge, in general terms, the effectiveness of the three existing media - paper, microfilm and online electronic transmission - and the newcomer CD-ROM in order to help establish which media are best suited to which areas of publishing.

6.2 Paper

Paper or papyrus has been with us since the earliest days of publishing when books were transcribed by hand on skins or parchment and it is what most of us are used to. Today, with the wide range of equipment and processes available to place information onto paper and package it, paper is an extremely versatile publishing medium and, of course, it is still by far the most widely used. We must now compare it against the criteria established above.

Storage capacity

Paper is a versatile medium. There is no bottom limit to the amount of information that can economically be distributed on paper - one line of text on a page is feasible - and while there is a limit to the storage capacity of an individual page, there is no limit to the number of pages we package together in a volume or series of volumes. However, there is a direct relationship between storage capacity, costs and space consumed. For each page of information we add there are additional production, consumable and distribution costs and a doubling in the bulk of the medium. Thus the limit to the storage capacity of paper is the amount which can be handled conveniently. Few of us would want to read a five thousand page novel in one volume or receive a hundred thousand page computer printout. If one measures storage capacity by the number of pages that can be stored in a particular storage area - one square foot - then clearly paper rates far behind microfilm or optical disks.

Type of material

There are very few limitations to the type of material that can be recorded onto paper. Text, graphics and colour material can be recorded onto paper and provided high quality paper is used, the resolution can be extremely high. Clearly paper is only a static medium, however, there is no provision for animation or motion video.

Ease of production

There are a vast range of techniques for producing and replicating material on paper ranging from simple photocopying systems to sophisticated offset lithography and laser printing systems. With paper, as with microfilm, the original material can come from one of two sources. In the first case the material is on a paper original and a direct copy of that original is simply transferred onto the required number of prints/copies via a photocopier or via a lithographic process. In the second case, the information is in digital form and can be output directly onto paper via a line or daisy wheel printer or one of a series of non-impact printers, most notably a laser printer.

Photocopying is the simplest and most convenient method of copying information held on paper provided quality is not a major consideration. There is no need to create a special master and in high volume the main cost element is the price of the paper and toner. If higher quality is required then there is a choice of laser printing and offset lithography. At present, laser printing is chiefly for textual material created on word processing systems but increasingly with the introduction of scanners and packaged desktop publishing systems, it is possible to create masters containing both graphics and text.

Ease of production with these systems depends on the volume of material being produced and the frequency of updates required. For a two or ten page report a photocopier or an offset lithography system is ideal, depending on the number of copies required. For a ten thousand page technical manual which needs updating every month there would be many benefits if the publisher were to capture the entire manual in digital form and design a sophisticated database structure which allowed for the text and graphics to be recalled, displayed, updated, merged and output in the required sequence on a regular basis. The alternative is to produce a plate for each page and use offset lithography

Cost of production and replication

As with any medium, there is a fixed cost involved in capturing and organising the information prior to placing it on paper, microfilm or CD-ROM or making it available online. With paper, if one is dealing with low volume simple reports, this cost can be considerably lower than for online or CD-ROM as all that is required, as illustrated above, is to copy the original using a photocopier or make a few plates and run off prints on a litho machine. Unless one is dealing with vast volumes, there is no requirement to go to the expense of designing and setting up a full computerised print database. If one is dealing with very large volumes of material, however, and wishing to update it on a regular basis and print it out via high speed laser printers then the steps that have to be gone through in capturing the material, coding it and organising the database, are almost exactly the same whether the final output is paper, microfiche, CD-ROM or online distribution.

Whether photocopying, offset lithography or laser printing is used, the basic cost element which does not change with paper systems is the cost of the paper and consumables such as toner/ink plus machine time and staff time supervising the operation. With paper the production and replication costs are directly geared to the number of pages which make up the publication or report. This is not the case, as we shall see below, with microfilm and CD-ROM.

Cost/ease of distribution

As with the production and replication process, one can state that the more pages there are the more expensive it will be to distribute them, both in terms of staff handling costs and fixed costs such as postal and transport rates. The bulkier a report is the costlier it is to distribute.

Turnaround times

Again, the flexibility of paper emerges here. If a single copy of a document is required the original can be photocopied in seconds or printed out on demand via a laser printer if it is held in machine readable form. However, as the volume of the material increases and the number of copies required goes up so the process of printing out, collating and despatching the material lengthens. Even here, however, 24 hour turnaround times are possible at a premium, e.g. the newspaper industry. Where turnaround times do suffer is if large reports have to be updated regularly and then distributed to large numbers of users via traditional postal routes.

Ease of updating

Updating of small volumes of printed material is a simple task, particularly if the material was created on a word processor and is available in coded form. However, as the volumes increase so there is a need to place the material into a database format where pages can be brought up in a predetermined sequence and updated and formatting and repagination can be done automatically.

Retrieval hardware

This is one of the great strengths of paper - it does not require any retrieval hardware so there is no expense involved, no compatibility problems and it can be read by everyone once they have found the required information. We deal with accessibility and portability below.

Portability

Related to the above, because no retrieval hardware is required and hence no power sources, paper is the most portable medium in most applications. For reading on a train or in bed, a book or newspaper is ideal and hence paper will remain unchallenged as a mass publishing medium. However, there are limits to the amount of printed material that can be carried and easily accessed. Vast stacks of computer printout are hardly portable. In the latter case portable microfiche readers or lap top computers could be more portable and convenient.

Accessibility of information

The structure of a paper product is determined by the author, publisher or printer or all three. Due to the fact that paper is basically a serial medium, bound into reports with a beginning, middle and end someone has to determine which order chapters will appear in or what sequence lists will be presented in and once they have done that it is fixed. The only way to cater for a wide range of retrieval requirements is to print the same list out in a number of diffferent sequences and this, of course, implies a cost and space overhead.

The structured nature of printed publications is, of course, not a problem in cases such as novels or even newspapers and magazines. With a novel most people want to read from the beginning to the end and with a newspaper most people want to browse and paper is ideal for both these purposes. However, if the information is aimed at multiple users who all want to access it in different ways then one structured sequence laid out on paper is unsatisafctory and one begins to need an electronic database format. As an example, bibliographic data can be organised by author, by title of book, by date or by subject category. Different users or even the same user will want to access the material by all of these parameters, probably more, so publishers are faced with producing five or six printed listings or offering the database online.

Ease of use

We are all brought up to accept paper and, by and large, it is what we are happiest with. We collect coffee table books and regard old books as works of art which have a value in themselves quite apart from their content.

However, moving away from the recreational area to the utility publishing sector where the only aim is to distribute information to people in an easily accessible form, books and other printed material clearly have some major limitations. Large multi-volume directories are intimidating and both physically and logically difficult to use. Again, as we pointed out before, the information is laid out in one sequence which may be extremely unhelpful for particular users and the printed indexes can often appear just as inflexible.

Integration with existing systems

Taking the example of a directory used above, not only is it difficult to use but also, there is no way in which the data extracted from the directory can be combined or reprocessed except by laboriously copying sections of the directory and keying them into a computer system. Information held in printed form cannot easily be re-entered into a computer system and with the growth of PCs in business and academic life there is a growing requirement, unmet by printed material, to take data from published sources and process it. The social researcher will want to take data from the census and build it into a model, the marketing man will want to take data from printed sources and build it into his spreadsheets. In those environments there is already a demand for electronic alternatives to paper publishing systems which can be more easily integrated into existing and developing PC based networks.

Summary

The main benefits of paper as a publishing medium are therefore, that there is no need for any retrieval hardware and hence it is a portable medium that can be easily used at home, in meetings and in the train. It is a also a versatile medium capable of holding text and high quality colour graphics and can be used to produce a small number of copies on a low volume copier or millions of copies via high speed printing machines. If required, 24 hour turnaround times can be achieved in high volume applications such as newspapers.

The main weaknesses are that each page of paper has a low storage capacity and paper becomes a very bulky and expensive medium for storing hundreds or thousands of pages of text or graphics. Distribution of large amounts of information on paper is also very expensive and cumbersome and turnaround times for large amounts of price sensitive material have to be measured in weeks if not months.

Finally, the information distributed on paper is often not easily accessible or usable because it is structured in one particular way and the material cannot be re-entered back into a computer system for reprocessing.

6.3   Microfilm

Microfilm was first used commercially in the 1920's when banks used 16mm roll film to film copies of all the cheques they received in case they were needed for evidence purposes. Libraries soon began to use 35mm roll microfilm to preserve old documents and reduce the space required to hold them and today scholarly microform publishing is a flourishing business. After the second world war, usage of microfilm grew steadily with a number of new formats being introduced. 35mm aperture cards were introduced to store images of engineering drawings, maps and plans, microfiche (strips of film measuring 105 x 148mm) were introduced as a convenient, easily replicated publishing medium and microfilm jackets were introduced as the microfilm equivalent of the updatable file folder. In the sixties we saw Computer Output Microfilm (COM) recorders, capable of taking data from computer systems and outputting it onto microfiche or roll film at high speed - providing an economical alternative to high speed computer printers - and in the seventies we have seen computer assisted microform retrieval systems introduced to improve the flexibility and responsiveness of microfilm filing systems in active filing environments.

Microfilm systems, like paper systems, can best be divided into two types. The first type - source document microfilm systems - are like photocopying systems, a paper original is filmed and copies of the miniaturised film are made and distributed as required. An example would be the microfilm version of The Times newspaper. Libraries who want back copies of The Times pay a subscription and receive a year's back issues on 35mm roll film. The original newspapers are filmed once and many thousands of copies are made from the original film and distributed to the subscribing libraries.

The second form of microform system, as described above, is COM. COM systems are the microfilm equivalent of laser printing systems in the paper world. To use COM the material must be in coded form. It is then output to a COM recorder either online or via magnetic tapes. Formatting and indexing data is included in the tape as it would be with a laser printing system. Indeed, many large organisations will have a COM recorder and laser printer connected up to their mainframe computers and output jobs onto microfilm or paper, depending on the distribution requirementsand size of job.

When microfilm systems first became popular in the 1960s we saw many euphoric articles predicting that all libraries would disappear and the publishing world would be revolutionised by the advent of microfilm. In the event microfilm has achieved widespread use and is now a $4 billion industry worldwide but it has actually had very little effect on the traditional publishing market for reasons we will see below. Now the same predictions are being made about CD-ROM and we have to wonder whether they will be equally wide of the mark or whether CD-ROM really will have the impact predicted for microfilm.

Storage capacity

One 100 foot roll of 16mm microfilm can store over 2,500 frames, each containing the image of an A3 or smaller page or some 4,000-5,000 frames, where each frame contains the image of an A5 or smaller document (e.g. a cheque). One A6 size source document microfiche stores 98 frames and one COM microfiche can store some 270-400 frames. Hence in pure storage terms, microfilm is a very compact medium. Studies have shown that in large scale systems microfilm can save some 95-98% of the space occupied by equivalent paper filing systems. However, whereas with paper systems one page can be copied and distributed conveniently and economically, with microfilm if only one page needs to be copied, an entire microfiche has to be produced or a strip of film has to be produced and loaded into a jacket. Hence, while the overall storage capacity of microfilm is good, microfilm is not as versatile as paper for distributing small amounts of information.

Type of material

Source document microfilm, like paper photocopying systems, can be used to capture all types of material - text, graphics and tonal material. However, just as a special type of photocopier is needed to copy colour material so with microfilm a special type of film - colour film from Ilford or Kodak - is needed to capture colour material and colour microfilming is a skilled job. Also, as with paper, microfilm is a static medium so there is no provision for reproducing motion video.

The quality of reproduction attainable with microfilm can be extremely high but typically is closer to that obtained through photocopying rather than in graphic art applications.

Ease of production

For in-house use where the originals are in paper form, microfilming, like photocopying, can be a fast and simple operation. High speed rotary cameras will film thousands of documents per hour and even with awkward material such as bound volumes and journals, rates of several hundred pages per hour can be sustained due to the fact that with microfilm, all that is required is for the camera shutter to open and the whole page is exposed in one movement.

There are two main points to note with microfilming. The first is that, unless you are just filming a book or a back-run of a journal, the documents have to be sorted into the desired order before they are filmed and that order is then fixed. The only alternative is to key in indexing data as the documents are filmed so they can be filmed at random and then accessed via a computer index. The second is that once the documents have been filmed the film has to be processed before it can be used. This results in a delay and necessitates staff trained in the use of chemicals.

Cost of production and replication

Source document filming is a relatively low cost operation. If 16mm roll film is used then commercial bureaux charge rates of £10-£20 per 1,000 frames to film the documents and process the film. With source document microfiche typical costs are £8-£15 for a 98 frame microfiche. For replication one 100 foot reel of 16mm roll film holding approximately 2,500 frames can be copied on diazo film for about £3-£6. One 98 frame microfiche can be copied onto diazo film for as little as 10-15 pence. Hence, for in-house use where large numbers of documents have to be filmed and only one or two copies are required, roll film is ideal. For publishing purposes where 500 copies of a 60 page report have to be distributed, microfiche is the ideal medium and combined production and replication costs are far lower than with paper.

A typical COM recorder costs in the region of £60,000-£150,000 so while there are some 300 installed in companies in the U.K., the majority of users tend to use a bureau service where they send their data to a bureau on tape and they print it out onto microfiche, copy the fiche and return the masters and the copies to the client. COM fiche are produced at higher reduction ratios than source document fiche so 208, 270 or even 400 frames can be recorded on one fiche. Production costs for a COM fiche range from £1.50 to £4 and duplication costs are the same as for source document fiche. It can be appreciated, therefore, that the costs of producing and replicating COM fiche are far lower than the cost of producing the same amount of material on paper via a laser printer. Hence COM has been widely used as a distribution medium.

Cost/ease of distribution

Due to its low production and replication costs and the compact nature of the medium, microfilm, in particular microfiche, has proved a very attractive distribution medium in in-house and technical publishing applications. Ten COM fiche or the equivalent of 2,700 pages can be distributed for the price of a first class stamp - a considerable saving in transport costs over paper. In addition, microfiche make an ideal medium for an on-demand print system. One master microfiche can be kept and as orders are received replicates are produced via a simple contact replication process, resulting in savings in warehouse space and dead stock.

Turnaround

With source document microfilming, as with photocopying, turnaround is a function of the size of the original document and the number of copies required. Replication is faster than any printing process with duplicators capable of producing 2,000-3,000 copy microfiche per hour, each containing 270 frames of information.

With COM, turnaround times can be even quicker as modern COM recorders can produce one 270 frame microfiche per minute and have integral processors which produce master microfiche ready for replication. Many microfiche based publishing services offer 24 hour turnaround times and even same day turnaround for a premium.

Ease of update

Updating is a limitation with a microform system. Once produced, master and replicate microfilms cannot be physically annotated and although specialised updatable filming processes do exist, even they require the use of a camera to update the original master microfiche, copy microfiche cannot be updated by users.

With source document microform publishing systems there is often no alternative but to completely refilm all the material, new and old on a regular basis and many microform publishers do this on a quarterly basis. With COM, it is possible to update a large database by simply printing out all the new material on one or more microfiche and then producing an amended index microfiche pointing to the new material but not to the outdated material.

Clearly microfilm, like paper is not the ideal way of disseminating highly volatile information that changes every minute or every hour - online is by far the best medium for such databases.

Retrieval hardware

Compared to paper, the fact that microform users need at least a reader and sometimes a reader-printer is a definite disadvantage for microfilm. In the early days of microfilm the readers left a lot to be desired, particularly roll film readers where reels of film had to be manually threaded on and wound through and the wet process printers were awkward to use and maintain and produced indifferent quality prints. Today, however, microprocessor controlled roll film retrieval units offer fast, accurate retrieval of the film and plain paper printers offer photocopy quality, low cost enlargements.

Clearly, however, whatever advances are made in the design of microfilm readers and reader-printers, the need for an optical reader means that they will never be widely accepted as a consumer medium and rival paper for the distribution of books and newspapers.

Portability

As stated above, microfilm has to be viewed via specific hardware and hence it is not as portable a medium as paper. In the sixties and early seventies companies spent millions trying to develop book size microfilm readers powered by batteries or solar energy but no-one has ever satisfactorily solved the problem of optically enlarging and displaying images stored on microfilm. Portable microfiche readers can be used in a car or at home but cannot easily be used on the train.

Accessibility

Traditional source document microfilm systems, like paper printing systems commit the publisher to selecting one or two sequences in which to order the material. As microfilm is a more compact, cheaper medium than paper, it is possible to print the same material in a number of sequences e.g. author/title/subject, but even with microfilm this represents a large overhead with major bibliographic listings such as British Books in Print or the British National Bibliography. In addition, because the microfilm only carries an image or a print frame, the information stored on the film cannot be searched on a full text basis, an increasing requirement with large databases.

Ease of use

As reported in the section on retrieval hardware, early microfilm readers and reader-printers were poor in design and reliability and led to considerable user resistance. Today many of the mechanical problems have been overcome but as the PC has become established so users are beginning to demand that the data they want be accessible online and fully searchable and hence there is still user resistance in many application areas.

Integration with existing systems

As stated above, microfilm, like paper, is not easily machine readable and hence, even with COM systems, once the data has been output onto microfiche, it cannot be read back into a computer and reprocessed. Hence, like paper, microfilm does not meet the needs of those PC users who wish to access selected segments of data from published sources and then download them into their PC for subsequent processing or modelling.

Summary

The main benefits of microfilm, therefore, as a distribution medium, are the relatively low cost and fast capture rates achievable, the fact that original material and coded data can be captured on the same medium, the very low replication and duplication costs, the relatively high storage capacity, the relatively low cost hardware required to read back the information and the fact that text, graphics and tonal/colour material can be captured.

The main disadvantages of microfilm, compared to paper are that it requires hardware to access it and hence is not fully portable. It cannot be easily annotated and it is not designed for distributing documents of a few pages.

The main disadvantages compared to online systems are that microfilm cannot be updated online, the only way to update a microfilm file is to refilm all or part of the file. Information on microfilm is also not always easily accessible - particularly by a number of users with different search requirements - as the data is output in a structured sequence which may not meet every users' requirements. Finally, and most significantly, information distributed on microfilm cannot be read back into computer systems for subsequent processing and hence microfilm does not adequately meet the needs of the growing number of computer users for a data distribution medium that allows them to download data from the distribution medium into their computer systems.

6.4   Online distribution

Online information systems began to be introduced in the early to mid 1970s. The U.K.'s Online Conference, organised by Learned Information, has just celebrated its 10th anniversary and now attracts some 3,000-4,000 delegates, underlining the widespread usage made of online distribution systems today. Essentially an online system comprises a file server system with one or more magnetic disks where the database is held, a host computer system and one or more end user terminals which may be within the same building and connected to the host via a local area network or in remote locations and connected to the host via a modem and a telephone line. As with paper and microfilm systems, therefore, online distribution can be used in-house for distributing corporate data, it can be used to link suppliers with dealers in technical publishing applications or it can be used to distribute information to end users on a commercial basis.

Storage capacity

Theoretically, there is no limit to the potential storage capacity of an online system. Realistically it is limited to the number of magnetic disk drives which can be controlled by one host and offer realistic response times and then the capacity of the disk drives themselves. It is sufficient to say, at present, that most textual databases can be accommodated on existing online systems but if suppliers wish to build up large graphic databases in future then optical storage systems and higher bandwidth networks will be needed.

There is, of course, a considerable cost involved in adding large numbers of high capacity magnetic disk drives to the system but this simply means that the database provider must be sure that, in the case of in-house systems, his database is valuable enough to the company to justify the expense or, in the case of commercial databases, is of sufficient interest to enough people to cover the costs of storing the data and make a reasonable profit. Clearly no-one is going to set up an online database just so one or two users can access it. In the case of a commercial database there must be a minimum number of users prepared to pay a considerable amount each year in order to access the database and in-house, usually there must be a need for a number of online database systems in order to jsutify setting up the necessary hardware and software.

Type of material

Most databases currently available are limited to text and numeric data but many now incorporate computer graphics and, via videotex interfaces, some companies are now experimenting with low resolution digitised photographic images. There is a limit, however, to how far images can be handled in online systems due to the fact that most external systems rely on telephone lines and data cannot be transmitted down them fast enough to support images and also to the fact that most online users use standard computer terminals and the monitors do not have the necessary resolution to support image display. Clearly with online systems, as with microfilm and paper, motion video cannot be supported.

Ease of production

As outlined in Chapter Three, setting up any database is a relatively complex exercise involving data capture, database design, indexing and loading. There is no real online equivalent to photocopying or source document microfilming where one simply copies an original - except perhaps if one counted electronic mail and facsimile as online distribution systems. With online, therefore, we are immediately looking at applications where a medium to large volume of information needs to be held centrally and updated regularly and where users need fast access to the data in coded, searchable form via their PCs or dedicated online terminals.

If we discount photocopying and source document microfilm systems then online distribution is being compared with using a laser printer to output a database onto paper prior to distribution, to COM where a database is output onto microfiche or to CD-ROM where the entire database or a sub-set of it is output onto CD-ROM and distributed to a user for local access. In these latter applications then the ease of production would be approximately the same for all four media and indeed, the same database can be output in all four ways if there is a requirement.

Cost of production/replication

Again, the same points apply here. The initial job of designing and creating the database is a complex task and represents a considerable overhead to the in-house or commercial publisher. However, once the database has been created then it can be updated online and maintenance is not excessive. Potential online information distributors can receive help and guidance in designing and creating the database from a number of system integrators and software suppliers and, if they lack the resources to market the database and the hardware to maintain it they can enlist the services of a host who will take the database, put it up on their host computer system and market it to their large number of existing clients. Again, therefore, as with paper and microfilm systems, there are bureau services available if the publisher simply wants to limit his activities to gathering and organising the data.

Cost/ease of distribution

The sale and marketing of online systems has proved difficult for many information providers and this explains the growth of the host companies who effectively take over that role and market the online databases to end users. If they are using a host then the information provider does not effectively have to worry about distribution at all - he produces one or two copies of the database and gives them to the host to put up on the system.

Turnaround

Clearly there is a lengthy turnaround between the decision to set up a large online database system and the actual implementation but once the system is set up then it can be updated relatively easily. With an in-house system the turnaround time is defined by how long it takes to capture the new data and process it so that it is in a form in which it can be added to the database. In the case of commercial systems it is the time it takes to capture and process the information plus the time it takes for the host to load the new data up onto the database. The latter may be daily, weekly or monthly, depending on the agreement between the host and the database provider and, ultimately, on the size and value of the database and the number of users of the online service.

Ease of update

This is one of the main advantages of online distribution and explains why all providers of volatile information have adopted it. Once the database has been set up, in-house users can update the system online as well as access it online so data can literally be updated in seconds and hence financial databases and airline seat booking systems all use online systems.

Retrieval hardware

Clearly, online users require a terminal and a modem and access to at least a telephone line. This restricts the use of online systems quite considerably at present. They cannot easily be used in a car, unlike microfilm or paper based systems, they cannot be used in a bus or train, unlike paper systems and they cannot easily be used in remote locations and the third world where telecommunication facilities are not available.

Portability

As described above, the retrieval equipment required to access online databases today is not very portable but with in-car telephones and improved telecommunications facilities in the future this limitation will become less significant.

Accessibility

Online scores very highly here as the databases are designed to aid accessibility and normally support structured and unstructured full text searches so the entire database can be searched. The only deterrents to use are the need to log on and go through various security procedures and the fact that, due to the use of telephone lines, interference can cause problems.

Ease of use

At present many end users of bibliographic databases need training in the search software and command systems that a particular database employs and if they need to access a number of databases this can be a deterrent. However, once the search strategies have been mastered the data is then far more accessible than via paper or microfilm based systems. Moreover, in specialised online services such as videotex based systems and a number of in-house databases, every effort is made to guide the user around the database and there are numerous help facilities which all aid the use of the system.

Integration

An online system can be easily integrated into current computer systems as the data is in coded form and sub-sets of data can be downloaded into the user's PC for subsequent processing. In some cases, of course, this will necessitate the payment of a fee.

Summary

The main benefits of online distribution systems, therefore, are firstly that the data is in coded form and hence is easily searchable and, provided the database has been well designed, can meet the needs of a wide range of users with different requirements. Secondly the data can be updated online so financial data is available within seconds and there is never any danger of users accessing out-of-date information. Thirdly, once the database has been designed and set up and the distribution mechanism is established, there are very few additional costs to the information provider (consumable costs, transport costs) and the user only pays on a usage basis. He does not have to purchase vast amounts of data on paper or film that he will never use because he has no way of telling what information will be used, he simply pays for what he accesses.

Fourthly, and finally, online systems are compatible with in-house PC systems so data retrieved from an online database can be downloaded and stored on a PC for subsequent processing.

The limitations of online systems include the fact that, in order to create a database the data must first be captured and converted into machine readable form - a considerable overhead - the database must then be designed and organised and finally, it must be up online via a host or in-house. Clearly, therefore, it is only applicable in certain cases where a relatively large store of valuable information needs to be accessed by a substantial body of users who are prepared to a pay a premium in order to gain fast access to it.

The second limitation concerns the fact that users must have a terminal, a modem and access to telecommunications facilities in order to access the databases and this further limits the range of applications for online systems.

Thirdly, there is a limit to the graphics which can be held and offered on an online system and currently that precludes the provision of high resolution facsimile images and any form of motion video.

Fourthly, users have to be trained to use the more complex databases and have to pay access both to the host on a time or hit basis and to the telephone company on a call basis.

6.5   CD-ROM Systems

Having established the strengths and weaknesses of paper, microfilm and online systems we must now remind ourselves briefly of the strengths and limitations of CD-ROM as a distribution medium so that we can place the four alternative media together in table form and provide an indication of the key qualiies of each medium which helps define the application areas it is best suited to.

Storage capacity

Each CD-ROM has a storage capacity of 550 Mbytes or, deducting 20% for indexing overheads, approximately 250,000 pages of coded text or 10,000 scanned images. This is an impressive figure and makes CD-ROM a far more compact medium than paper or COM and approximately twice as compact as roll microfilm for the storage of images.

However, the very storage density of CD-ROM means that it does not compete with paper as a way of distributing a few pages of information nor microfiche as a way of distributing thirty or forty pages of information. The mastering costs associated with CD-ROM and the hardware costs associated with accessing the data stored on CD-ROM mean that it will not be cost effective for distributing less than 1,000 to 2,000 pages of information or approximately 5 microfiche or 10-20 Mbytes and will not really come into its own until one is distributing 10,000 pages of information. CD-ROM, in that sense, is like microfilm, it is an incremental medium.

Type of material

CD-ROM currently is primarily being used to store text and computer graphics but, as we have seen in this report, CD-ROM and other CD systems can be used to store audio information, raster scanned images, video and full motion video so inherently it is the most flexible of the distribution media in terms of the type of material it can hold. However, against that one has to consider that at present CD-ROM drives are being attached to PCs with low resolution screens and to distribute raster scanned images it would be necessary to use more expensive high resolution display units so there is a difference between what is technically possible and what is cost effective at present.

Ease of production

As outlined in Chapter Three, the stages involved in the production of a CD-ROM are similar to those involved in producing an online database and in some cases more complicated as develpers work out their own proprietary file structures. In the future, as the High Sierra Group Standard is adopted, the process will be simplified somewhat and at a basic level we could just see companies using CD-ROM in-house to distribute files but to make full use of CD-ROM as with online distribution, it is essential to go through the expensive one time process of creating a database. Again, this limits CD-ROM to applications requiring the distribution of large amounts of information to large numbers of end users with a regular update cycle and where the information is valuable enough for the end users to pay a premium for the service.

Cost of production and replication

Again, we have seen that the cost of creating the database is a movable figure which currently ranges from £10,000-£100,000 depending on how much data capture needs to be done, how big the database is and how complex the database structure needs to be. The fixed costs are the mastering costs which are approximately £2,000-3,000 per CD-ROM and the replication costs which, depending on the number of discs being replicated, range from £5-£30 per disc.

The other key factor here is that whereas large and medium size companies can create printed publications, microfilm publications and even online databases in-house, it will not be possible for even the largest companies to master CD-ROMs in-house or to replicate them in-house as the cost of a CD-ROM mastering and replicating facility is in the region of £50-100 million. This will have implications on turnaround times and could limit the usage of CD-ROM where security is an issue.

Cost/ease of distribution

Again, as we have seen, the cost of the replicates goes down the more discs are made and with the database creation and mastering costs being one time costs clearly the economics of CD-ROM become more attractive the more potential users there are. This reinforces the point that CD-ROM does not compete with photocopying or microform as a means of distributing small numbers of a report, it is rather geared to distributing large numbers of medium to large size databases to end users. In terms of ease of distribution, CD-ROM is a very compact medium and hence postage costs will be low and if the disc is full the consumable costs are also relatively low at £10-£20 for 200,000 pages.

Turnaround times

Here CD-ROM certainly cannot compete with online systems. There will be a delay while the database is updated, the tapes are sent to the mastering facility, the check disk is produced, replicates are stamped and checked and then sent either to end users or to the publisher for distribution. It is unlikely that anyone will be able to sustain a largescale CD-ROM publishing activity with more than a monthly turnaround cycle. If they do it will not mean that the data is a week old, it will simply mean that data is being prepared in advance and distributed on a weekly basis.

The only exception to this could be for relatively small scale in-house applications where companies such as 3M with their replication technique, can offer two or three day turnaround of limited numbers of replicates. With that type of service in-house users could manage a weekly update service.

Such turnaround times are not even competitive with COM microfiche in many applications. In in-house applications, COM can provide a 24 hour or even six hour turnaround and even in largescale applications, such as the banks, COM fiche are distributed to thousands of branches every day.

Ease of update

As described above, CD-ROM on its own is not suited to distributing volatile information that is changing every minute of every day. CD-ROM is a physical medium, like microfiche or paper and is read only. Once the CD-ROM has been produced it cannot physically be changed. The only way to update a CD-ROM database is to reissue it. Hence the time taken to prepare the database, ship it to a mastering facility, master the database, produce the required number of replicates and distribute them will define the turnaround times offered by CD-ROM and hence the number and frequency of updates that can be produced. The only way in which this limitation can be overcome is to offer a combined CD-ROM and online service where backfiles of static information are made available on CD-ROM and volatile information is accessed online.

Retrieval hardware

As we have seen the minimum configuration at present is a PC plus a CD-ROM drive and the relevant interface and it will take a year before standards are accepted and the economics of mass production push down the price of CD workstations from the current price of approx £3,000 including the PC to a possible £1,000. The alternative will be for dedicated CD-ROM workstations such as the proposed CD-I player to lead the way in cost reductions.

The main benefit that CD-ROM has is that PCs are selling in vast quantities so for many users CD-ROM will be just another add-on peripheral and will be justified as soon as a valuable publication they need to access becomes available on CD-ROM.

Portability

Currently, a PC with a CD-ROM drive is not very portable but when half height 5.25 inch drives become available we may see purpose built knee-top CD-ROM workstations which would at least be as portable as microfiche readers.

Accessibility of information

This is potentially the main benefit that CD-ROM will bring as they will combine the searchability of online databases with the many advantages that local access can bring - namely the ability to handle graphics and motion video on specialised workstations, unlimited access without time penalties and the ability to offer the user far more help facilities than is currently practical with online systems.

Already many companies are working on end user interfaces for CD-ROM systems and systems that will offer multi-level software so experienced users and novice users can be catered for on one system. Potentially, also one can have several databases on one CD-ROM accessible via one set of retrieval software so lessening the need for end user training in a number of different systems.

Ease of use

Here again CD-ROM looks set to score over paper, microfilm and online systems. Once standards are agreed the logging on process will be simpler than for online systems and typically a user will switch his CD-ROM system on once and then leave it on for the rest of the day. There will be scope for considerably more help facilities on a CD-ROM than on an online system including tutorial sequences designed to introduce the user to the system.

Integration with existing systems

Here CD-ROM is really set to score over Computer Output Microfilm and paper based systems. Data distributed on CD-ROM can be read back into PCs for subsequent processing so, for example, bibliographic data distributed on CD-ROM could form the basis of an online ordering system or an online catalogue card or online catalogue record creation service. In a second example, if directories are distributed on CD-ROM then sets of company addresses can be selected, downloaded onto magnetic media and used as the basis for mailing lists. The only alternative with paper or microfilm directories would be to transcribe manually the information and key it into a PC system.

Summary

The main benefits of CD-ROM when compared to paper and microfilm distribution systems are firstly, for the distribution of high volumes of information where the high storage density and low replication costs of CD-ROM make it cost effective. Secondly, the fact that the data is in coded form means that, provided the database has been well designed, the data is more easily searchable and can satisfy the search requirements of a wide range of different users. Thirdly, since CD-ROMs are computer peripherals and data is stored on them in coded form, data retrieved from a CD-ROM can be downlaoded and stored on PCs for subsequent processing.

The main benefits of CD-ROM when compared to online systems are due to the fact that the CD-ROM is distributed for local use so there are no telecommunications costs and no limitations placed on the type of material which can be stored or the amount of help facilities made available by the bandwidth of the telephone line connecting the user to the online host. With CD-ROM both images, text, audio and data can be stored on one medium and with CD-I and the forthcoming CD-Video format, even still frame and motion video can be supported.

Secondly, CD-ROMs could be sold on a yearly subscription basis, simplifying budgets for information users who, after paying a one time subscription, are then free to access the CD-ROM as often as they like with incurring extra costs.

7.   COMPARISON WITH OTHER OPTICAL PUBLISHING SYSTEMS

In the previous chapter we looked back and compared CD-ROM with the main traditional information distribution systems. Here we want to look forward briefly and compare CD-ROM with some of the alternative optical media currently available or under development. In Chapter One we placed CD-ROM in context and compared it with CD-Interactive so we will not include the other forms of compact disc here. We will briefly compare CD-ROM with four other optical media - OROMs, hybrid videodiscs, optical cards and WORM (Write Once Read Many times) discs.

7.1   OROM

The key advantages of CD-ROM as a publishing medium, as we have seen, are standardisation, high storage capacity, the availability of mastering and replication facilities and relatively low cost hardware.

One drawback with CD-ROM is its use of CLV mode recording which results in relatively slow access times of 1-2 seconds in current CD-ROM drives. A second potential drawback is that in addition to using CLV format, the CD-ROM is 12 cm or 4.72 inches in diameter and hence is not compatible with the emerging 5.25 inch WORM disks and prototype 5.25 inch erasable optical disks which tend to use the CAV format.

A number of companies have therefore floated the concept of a 5.25 inch CAV mode read only optical disk - variously termed OROM or DataROM - which could play in a new generation of multifunction 5.25 inch optical disk drives capable of accepting read only, write once and erasable optical disks. The benefits of OROM would be that it was compatible with future optical media standards, had faster access times and data transfer rates, would be easily adaptable to higher storage densities as they became feasible and would serve the high end computer marketplace where multi-user access was a requirement, leaving the low end publishing marketplace to CD-ROM.

One of the first companies to float the idea of OROM was 3M who, in co-operation with Optimem showed a prototype multifunction 5.25 inch drive in the U.S. and have agreed to co-operate in a collaborative venture where Optimem produces the drive and 3M produces the media. Their aim is to get agreement on a single media format for all three forms - read only, write once and erasable. In the ptototype system, the discs had a storage capacity of 200 Mbytes per side; access times of 100 msecs and data transfer rates of 5 Mbits per second.

Independently of this announcement, a spokesman from Sony announced in June 1985 at a Technology Opportunity Conference organised by Rothchild Consultants in the U.S. that they are developing a read only optical disk which they are calling DataROM, which will use a compatible format to their write once and erasable optical disks and will permit write once, erasable and read only data on the same disk and provide faster access and data transfer rates than CD-ROM. For Sony the DataROM will also be 5.25 inches or 13cm in diameter, use sectorised data and serve the high end market where multi-user access is important, leaving the low end single user access, electronic publishing marketplace to CD-ROM.

A third key player in this field is, of course, Philips, who have different divisions to serve the many different markets from the domestic consumer market for CD-I and CD Audio through to the mainstream computer market for write once, erasable and OROM media. Philips are committed to CD-ROM and CD-I for the domestic consumer and low end electronic publishing marketplace but Laser Magnetic Storage, the Philips and Control Data Corporation subsidiary, are putting the finishing touches to a write once 5.25 inch drive that will also accept OROM disks prepared to the same format.

It would appear, therefore, from these and similar announcements, that there is a market for a faster, higher performance read only optical disk that will be upwardly compatible with planned 5.25 inch WORM and erasable disk formats. It is widely believed that this is the type of optical product that IBM is primarily interested in supporting - a view that was strengthened by a recent meeting of the U.S. National Information Standards Organisation held to discuss the proposed High Sierra Group CD-ROM File Format Standard. At this meeting, held in New York in October 1986, a spokesman for IBM queried the fact that the standard referred to a product - namely CD-ROM - and a motion was put and passed that all references to CD-ROM should be removed from the standard and replaced with the term read only optical disks. The reason given for this action was that the Philips/Sony Yellow Book was not freely available in the public domain but many interpreted the move as IBM wishing to make it clear that the standard could be applied to other CAV format OROMs if required.

Assuming that drives are produced that will support OROM disks and that IBM and others endorse this medium, what effect would OROM have on CD-ROM?

The answer would appear to be very little at this stage for commercial publishers keen to launch CD-ROM products apart from creating further confusion and hence delaying purchasing decisions still further. In commercial publishing applications, the emphasis will be on low cost workstations, standards and the widespread availability of mastering and replicating facilities and data preparation facilities. CD-ROM already is meeting these requirements.

Similarly, for many technical publishing applications where CD-ROM is in competition with existing paper and microfiche based systems, the key requirements will be low cost workstations and low replication costs for the media.

However, for software distribution and the distribution of raw data and graphics libraries for use in particular computer systems and for a number of in-house data distribution applications then OROM looks potentially very attractive and if it receives the right backing from IBM and others it will be widely adopted by mainstream computer users.

OROM will offer multi-user access, compatibility with other formats, faster access and faster data transfer rates and where it is used for distributing software, documentation and graphics libraries then the possible shortage of mastering facilities and even lack of standards will not prove a significant drawback. 3M can master OROM media already and if OROM receives the backing of major computer companies then many current mastering facilities can be adapted to produce and replicate OROM discs.

Clearly, much of what we have said in this section is only speculation and the fact is that today there are no standards for OROM or DataROM and 3M and Sony are proceeding on their own with little consultation. Nevertheless, we feel that announcements will be made over the next year and we wanted to cover OROM here to give an indication of where we feel it will fit into the general range of publishing and distrinution alternatives outlined in this report. We feel it will be a high end product meeting the data distribution needs of mainstream computer users. It will not seriously challenge the embryonic CD-ROM marketplace for distributing commercial databases, reference works and images to PC users.

7.2   Hybrid videodiscs

We referred to hybrid videodiscs very briefly in Chapter One in the section on videodiscs. When videodiscs were first launched as an analogue storage medium for the domestic consumer marketplace, many companies such as Reference Technology, Laserdata and TMS (all of whom are now major players in the CD-ROM marketplace) saw the potential of videodiscs and, by implication, all high density optical read only media, for data distribution or optical publishing as it has come to be known.

They developed techniques for encoding digital data within the video signal of the videodisc and set about developing their own proprietary optical publishing systems based around videodiscs. In these systems the publisher sent his database in coded form to one of the above companies and they encoded the data, recorded it on videodisc and produced replicate discs containing the digital data. For playback the user then needed an industrial videodisc player linked to a decoder/control unit which in turn was linked to a microcomputer. The data was then read off the videodisc, converted in real time from analogue to digital format, underwent an error detection and correction routine and was displayed on the computer screen.

These systems were called hybrid videodisc systems because they recorded digital data in the video format and it was theoretically possible to combine both analogue and digital data on the same videodisc, providing a hybrid system that could support still frame and motion video, text, data, graphics and audio.

The work of Laserdata, Reference Technology and the other suppliers is described in more detail in Cimtech Publication 23 (1) which also contains bibliographies for those who wish to study developments in this field in more detail. The main problem for all the suppliers of hybrid systems was the lack of standards in the field. All the suppliers used different techniques to encode their data, different hardware and different error detection and correction systems with the result that there was no interchangeability of discs and players and the large commercial publishers did not feel confident that any one supplier would triumph. In addition, due to the proprietary nature of the hardware and software used in the systems, prices were too high to make hybrid systems attractive to the generic publishing market.

The result is that hybrid systems only served a relatively specialist market and in the future, with CD-ROM available and CD-I on the horizon, the main applications where hybrid videodiscs will be used are where high storage densities are required (one videodisc can store in excess of 1 Gbyte of data) or where a mixture of high quality motion video and digital data is required.

Recently, Philips have announced their own hybrid videodisc which they call Laservision ROM which differs markedly from the earlier hybrid systems described above. With Laservision ROM Philips have not attempted to store data in the 55,000 video frames on each side of the disc - these are reserved for still frame or motion video. However, they have devised a technique for recording data in the twin audio tracks on a disc and claim that if no audio is required they can store some 324 Mbytes of data on each side of a 12 inch videodisc plus 55,000 video frames.

Laservision ROM was developed specifically for the BBC for use in their Domesday Project where they have placed a combination of still frame and moving video on a total of 165,000 frames on three sides of a videodisc and a combination of audio commentary and digital data on the audio tracks - providing close to 1 Gbyte of data on the three sides of the videodiscs.

Clearly the BBC could not have used CD-ROM or even CD-I to produce their electronic Domesday Book as they had a major requirement for motion video sequences and Philips believe that there are many more applications where a combination of high quality video plus data are required on the same disc. However, the Laservision ROM hardware is inevitably more expensive than current CD-ROM drives and it is difficult to see how, unless the government decide to subsidise the hardware, the BBC's original goal of making the Domesday discs available in all schools will be achieved.

In conclusion, therefore, we feel that hybrid videodisc systems, including Laservision ROM, will remain a rather specialist product for publishers and users with a strong requirement to use motion video and will have little impact on CD-ROM as a means of distributing data, text and computer generated or raster graphics.

7.3 Optical cards

Much has been written over the past few years about a related optical medium - the Drexon lasercard developed by Drexler Corporation. The Drexon laser cards, like optical disks can be read only or write once and are basically plastic credit cards with the optical recording medium applied in a strip as a replacement to the magnetic strip used in other so called smart cards. Drexler have sold non-exclusive licences for the technology to over thirty major companies worldwide in a bid to get the optical lasercard accepted as a worldwide standard and a number of applications have been announced for the cards, e.g. the Blue Cross Blue Shield applications where clients' medical details are recorded on read only cards and hospitals are issued with card readers for reading the data into IBM PCs.

A Drexon recording strip measuring 35 x 80mm has a storage capacity of 2 Mbytes and versions with storage capacities up to 10 Mbytes have been shown. The cards are wallet sized like a standard credit card and are fully encapsulated in polycarbonate plastic for security and usability. The Drexon cards can be prerecorded in the factory for Read Only Memory applications where many copies of permanent identical data are required, e.g. for distributing software programmes to personal computers. Drexler make use of high speed photolithography for mass production of the ROM cards using specialised equipment in cleanroom conditions and the data bits recorded on the cards are read using photodetector arrays. Drexler claim that in high volume read only laser cards could cost as little as $5.

The recordable laser cards also have a storage capacity of 2 Mbytes or approximately 800 pages of standard text. In addition to cardholder data and transaction information the cards could be used to store digitised photographs or fingerprints, encryption codes and a range of other deterrents against counterfeiting and other fraudulent uses of lost or stolen credit cards. The cards will be laser recordable at a secure point of issue or at point of use for cumulative record keeping or debiting and a standard blank recordable card could sell for roughly $2 in high volume.

A key element in the success of the cards will be the cost of the reading/writing equipment and its reliability. A number of Japanese companies have demonstrated both card readers and card reader-writers including Toshiba, Nipponcoinco, Canon and Olympus. Prices for these units will be a factor of volume and the first applications call for high volumes of both readers and read/write units. The Toshiba reader measures 150 x 210 x 290mm and offered a transfer speed of 32-64 Kbits per second. It uses a CCD array to read the data and is expected to be OEM priced at about £100. The reader/writer unit, capable or recording up to 2 Mbytes onto a card, measures 150 x 135 x 250mm and offers a write speed of 10 Kbits per second and a read speed of 64-128 Kbits per second. It is priced at approximately £1,500.

Clearly, given the low storage capacity of the cards and the relatively slow read speeds, optical cards are not going to challenge CD-ROMs for the distribution of high volume databases and indeed, the degree of overlap between CD-ROM and laser cards will be very small indeed. Now that we have an ever growing number of PC users we will see many and varied techniques devised to enable data to be distributed cost effectively to PC users. CD-ROM is for publishing complete databases and large volumes of text and graphics. Laser cards will be useful for distributing simple software packages to PC users or possibly for updating material distributed on CD-ROM. The prime applications, however, will be in the transaction handling environment.

7.4   WORM disks

In Chapter One, Section Three we identified two key application areas for WORM disks - as a data archiving medium in competition with magnetic tape and for the storage of facsimile scanned images of documents in competition with microfilm. Current 12 inch WORM disks and forthcoming high storage capacity 14 inch disks from Kodak and others will be used in large centralised systems and clearly there will be very litle overlap here between WORM disks and CD-ROM systems. In many applications textual and image databases will be captured and maintained on large WORM disks and then sub-sets of the databases will be downloaded onto CD-ROM for distribution and sale.

However, there are a growing number of 5.25 inch WORM drives coming onto the marketplace too and although these will be used to provide PC users with data archiving facilities and as part of PC based personal filing systems, one of the key application areas for such WORM disks could be the distribution of selected in-house databases and here WORM disks could compete with CD-ROM systems, depending on the number of end users and the need to update the information.

In the previous chapter we compared CD-ROM with microfilm and specifically with Computer Output Microfilm for the distribution of in-house databases and technical documentation. Many of the in-house applications of Computer Output Microfilm involved distributing from 1-10 copies of a database to specific workers within an organisation. The reason for doing it is that it is quicker and simpler for those users to access the data from COM fiche structured to meet their requirements than it is for them to access the database online in the form in which it is held on the mainframe and where they are in contention with other users.

With such a small number of end users CD-ROM would not be cost effective and could not offer the immediate turnaround of COM systems but WORM disks could provide a solution. The particular sub-set of the database required by the end users would be downloaded onto a 5.25 inch WORM disk and the required number of copies of the disk could be produced by serially copying disk to disk and the disks then distributed to the end users for access on their PCs. Currently it takes about 40 minutes to serially copy one side of a 200 Mbyte WORM disk and this time will come down as the raw error rates of the medium improve and as data transfer rates are increased. The benefits for users would, of course, be that the database remained in coded form and hence would be more easily searchable and processable.

Hence, in applications where the number of end users does not justify the cost of mastering a CD-ROM or where the turnaround times offered by CD-ROM are not acceptable or where, for security reasons, users do not wish to use external mastering and replication facilities, WORM disks could and, indeed, are already being used to replicate and distribute databases.

Companies who have already demonstrated such systems include MARCIVE in the U.S. who distribute bibliographic databases to libraries on 5.25 inch WORM disks and a company called Teletrak who have developed a complete Computer Output Optical Disk system designed to challenge current in-house COM systems.

With the Teletrak system companies produce a print tape, formatted exactly as if they were going to load it on their COM recorder and download the data onto Computer Output Microfiche. The tapes are loaded but instead of being displayed on a CRT and recorded onto film, the print image data is recorded onto 5.25 inch WORM disks using a software package developed by Teletrak and indexing data is created and stored on a hard disk. The double-sided 5.25 inch WORM disks hold 400 Mbytes of data or the equivalent of 70,000 computer report pages, 1,100 floppy diskettes or 300 COM microfiche and they can be copied and distributed for access by specific user departments.

We expect to see considerable developments in the area of WORM based systems for data distribution, image filing and data archiving in the next 12 months and clearly WORM disks will complement CD-ROM systems, enabling users to distribute databases to a relatively few end users. WORM disks will not be attractive in the commercial publishing environment or in high volume technical publishing applications as it will not prove practical to serially copy high volumes of WORM disks and the media and drive costs will be higher than for CD-ROMs.

Hence, looking at the main alternative optical media - OROMs, hybrid videodiscs, optical cards and WORM disks - we must conclude that while most of them look set to complement CD-ROM in future and fill some of the gaps in the maketplace which CD-ROM does not meet, none of them really pose a serious threat to CD-ROM in its chosen role as a low cost distribution medium for PC users which looks set to open up a mass marketplace for optical publishing systems. The closest competitor will be the OROM if it is adopted and promoted by IBM and other computer giants but, as I hope I have shown, even OROM would not be a direct competitor to CD-ROM for PC users who want a low cost distribution medium. It is a high end system with faster access rates and transfer rates which could meet the needs of the next generation of more powerful, multi-user PC systems, minicomputer users and mainframe users who will want to have fast conenvenient access to the vast amounts of data that can be distributed on optical media.

CD-ROM is here to stay and just as a comparison of CD-ROM with existing distribution media suggests many promising application areas where CD-ROM will prove indispensible, so a comparison with other optical media confirms that CD-ROM has a definite long term future as a publishing medium.

8. COMPANIES PROVIDING CD-ROM HARDWARE AND SERVICES

In this section we simply want to list the names and addresses of companies who are supplying CD-ROM hardware and services. As time goes on and the market stabilises so the number of companies coming into the CD-ROM field will increase and the infrastructure of drive and interface suppliers, retrieval software suppliers, data preparation services and mastering and replication facilities will stabilise. At this point, while it is possible to list drive suppliers, it is difficult to differentiate between those companies who simply supply indexing and retrieval software that can be used to prepare CD-ROM databases, those companies who provide data preparation services and those companies who will take responsibility for all the stages involved in producing a CD-ROM product from data capture to distribution of the replicated discs. Typically the latter companies will have contracted with a software supplier and will arrange with a mastering and replication facility to use their services.

To avoid confusion therefore, and the risk of offence to suppliers we shall group the software suppliers, data preparers and system integrators under the general heading of data preparers/system integrators. We shall not attempt to list current mastering and replication facilities but rather refer potential CD-ROM publishers to the data preparers/system integrators listed below who will be able to recommend one or other mastering and replication facility.

8.1 CD-ROM drive suppliers

Here we list manufacturers of CD-ROM drives, the model numbers of the drives that they have shown and their U.K. address where known.

Denon - DRD 550 CD-ROM drive
Denon America, 27 Law Drive, Fairfield, NJ 07006, U.S.A.

Hitachi New Media Products - CDR 1502S, 2500, 2500S
Hitachi Sales (U.K.) Ltd., Hitachi House, Hayes, Middlesex UB3 4DR, U.K.

JVC - developing CD-ROM drives - model names not available
JVC Corporation, 41 Slater Drive, Elmwood Park, NJ 07407, U.S.A.

Panasonic (Matsushita) - SQ D-100
Panasonic, 1 Panasonic Way, Secaucus, NJ 07094, U.S.A.

Philips - CDX-1000, CM 100, CM 110
Philips Electronics, City House, 420/430 London Road, Croydon, Surrey CR9 3QR, U.K.

Laser Magnetic Storage (a subsidiary of Philips & Control Data Corporation), P.O. Box 218, Building SA11-5, Eindhoven, Netherlands.

Sanyo - developing CD-ROM drives - model names not available
Sanyo Electric, 1200 West Artesia Blvd., Compton, CA 90220, U.S.A.

<u>Sony - CDU 100, CDU 200, CDU 5002</u>
Sony Corporation, Sony House, South Street, Staines, Middlesex, U.K.

<u>Toshiba - XM 2000</u>
Available in U.K. from DataGuild Ltd., Unit 9, The Pines Trading Estate, Broad Street, Guildford, Surrey GU3 3BH, U.K.

8.2   <u>Data preparers/system integrators</u>

<u>Europe</u>

Archetype Systems Ltd., 91/93 Charterhouse Street, London EC1M 6LN, U.K.

Battelle Institut E.V. Abt Software Products, Postfach 900160, Frankfurt, West Germany

Battelle Institute Ltd., 15 Hannover Square, London W1R 9AJ, U.K.

Bertelsmann AG, Carl Bertelsmann Street 161, Guertersloh 05241801, West Germany

BRS Europe, 73-75 Mortimer Street, London W1N 7TB, U.K.

CEDROM Technologies, 68 Quai de la Seine, 75019 Paris, France

Digital Equipment Corporation, CD-ROM Marketing, Engineering Division, P.O. Box 121, Imperial Way, Reading, Berks., U.K.

Elanders, P.O. Box 10238, S-43401 Kungsbacka, Sweden

Harwell (STATUS), Marketing and Sales Department, A.E.R.E., Harwell Laboratory, Oxfordshire OX11 ORA, U.K.

Logica Communications & Electronic Systems Ltd., 64 Newman Street, London W14 4SE, U.K.

Office Workstations Ltd. (OWL), 2 Easter Road, Edinburgh, Scotland

Pergamon Infoline (Compact Solution), 12 Vandy Street, London EC2A 2DE, U.K.

Philips Electronics, City House, 420/430 London Road, Croydon, Surrey CR9 3QR, U.K. (Laser Magnetic Storage, P.O. Box 218, Building SA11-5, Eindhoven, Netherlands

Scientific Consulting, Volkhovener Weg 172-176, 5000 Koln 71, West Germany

Silver Platter Information Ltd., 10 Barley Mow Passage, Chiswick, London W4 4PH, U.K.

STET, 00198 Roma, C So D'Italia, 858430, Italy

North America

Access Innovations, P.O. Box 40130, 4320 Mesa Grande SE, Albuquerque, NM 87196, U.S.A.

AMTEC Information Services, 3700 Industry Avenue, Lakewood, CA 90714-6050, U.S.A.

Battelle Software Products Center, 505 King Avenue, Columbus, OH 43201-2693, U.S.A.

BRS, 1200 Route 7, Latham, NY 12110, U.S.A.

Computer Access Corporation, Suite 324, 26 Brighton Street, Belmont, MA 02178-4008, U.S.A.

Cuneiform Inc., 11 Murphy Drive, Nashua, NH 03062, U.S.A.

Digital Equipment Corporation, 2 Mt Royal Ave, Marlborough, MA 01752, U.S.A.

Group L, 481 Carlisle Drive, Herndon, VA 22070, U.S.A.

Knowledgeset Corporation, 2511 Garden Road, Bldg C, Monterey, CA 93940, U.S.A.

Laserdata, One Kendall Square, Building 200, Cambridge, MA 02139, U.S.A.

Microsoft, 16011 N E 36th Way, Box 97017, Redmond, WA 98073-9717, U.S.A.

Microtrends Inc., 650 Woodfield Dr., Ste 730, Schaumburg, IL 60195, U.S.A.

NCR Corp., 292 Madison Avenue, New York, NY 10017, U.S.A.

Online Computer Systems, 20251 Century Boulevard, Germantown, MD 20874, U.S.A.

Reference Technology Inc., 5700 Flatiron Parkway, Boulder, CO 80301, U.S.A.

Reteaco Inc., 716 Gordon Baker Road, Willowdale, Ontario M2H 3B4, Canada

TMS Inc., 110 West 3rd Street, P.O. Box 1358, Stillwater, Oklahoma, 74076, U.S.A.

9. PROTOTYPE AND COMMERCIAL CD-ROM PRODUCTS

The aim of this report is to provide an introduction to CD-ROM and assess its potential as a publishing and data distribution medium. There is not space available to provide a comprehensive directory of CD-ROM projects and products and to do so would duplicate work being done by other companies who are assembling directories. We cannot possibly list all the companies who are considering or actually using CD-ROM for in-house and technical publishing applications. The list is substantial and includes government departments, public sector agencies and commercial companies. We outlined some of the most promising application areas in Chapter Five but readers requiring more detailed information on specific in-house CD-ROM projects are invited to contact the data preparers listed above.

Moving to the commercial publishing arena, one has to differentiate between companies who have produced a prototype CD-ROM disc to evaluate the technology and those companies who have launched or committed themselves to launching a commercial CD-ROM product. The initial list is endless and the value of such lists is questionable until the publishers actually commit themselves unless you are in a similar line of business and would like to contact the publisher concerned to learn his attitude to CD-ROM. Two newsletters which report on all new and proposed CD-ROM projects are the U.S. 'CD Data Report' (1) and the U.K.'s 'Optical Data Systems'.

The list of available commercial CD-ROM products is considerably shorter but there is already a directory of such products (3) available from Learned Information.

Here we will confine ourselves to listing a selection of CD-ROM products which the publishers have either made available commercially or have committed to making available commercially in 1987. We would recommend anyone interested in publishing material on CD-ROM to contact either the publishers or the data preparers involved in these projects to learn more about the products and the lessons that have been learned in their preparation.

Reference works/directories

1. 'Post Code Directory'. Publisher: British Post Office. Data Preparation: Silver Platter. Launch date 1986.

2. 'International Encyclopaedia of Education'. Publisher: Pergamon. Data Preparation: Pergamon Infoline (Compact Solution). Launch date 1987.

3. 'Maritime Commerce and Law'. Publisher: Publishers Database. Launch date 1987.

4. 'Academic American Encyclopaedia'. Publisher: Grolier. Data Preparation: Knowledgeset/PDSC. Launch date 1985.

5. 'Encyclopaedia of Science and Technology'. Publisher: McGraw-Hill. Launch date 1987.

Library/bookseller databases

6.   'Books in Print Plus'. Publisher: R. R. Bowker. Launch date 1986.

7.   'Ulrich's Plus'. Publisher: R. R. Bowker. Launch date 1986.

8.   'Any-Book'. Publisher: The Library Corporation. Launch date 1985.

9.   'LC MARC'. Publisher: The Library Corporation. Launch date 1985.

10. 'LISA (Library & Information Science Abstracts). Publisher: The Library Association. Data Preparer: Silver Platter. Launch date 1987.

11. 'British Books in Print'. Publisher: Whitakers. Launch date 1987.

Scientific and medical databases

12. 'PsycLIT'. Publisher: American Psychological Association. Data Preparer: Silver Platter. Launch date 1986.

13. 'Drugdex/Emergindex/Identidex/Poisindex'. Publisher: Micromedex. Launch date 1985.

14. 'Agricultural Database'. Publisher: Commonwealth Agricultural Bureau. Launch date 1987.

Financial/commercial databases

15. 'Corporate Database'. Publisher: Datext. Launch date 1985.

16. 'Compact Disclosure'. Publisher: Disclosure. Launch date 1985.

17. 'One Source'. Publisher: Lotus Information Services. Launch date 1986.

Addresses of publishers

American Psychological Association, Psychological Abstracts Information Services, 1400 North Uhle Street, Arlington, VA 22201, U.S.A.

R. R. Bowker, 205 East 42nd Street, New York, NY 10164, U.S.A.

Datext Inc., 444 Washington Street, Woburn, MA 01801, U.S.A.

Disclosure Inc., 5161 River Road, Bethesda, MD 20816, U.S.A.

Grolier Electronic Publishing, 95 Madison Avenue, New York, NY 10016, U.S.A.

Library Association Publishing Ltd., 7 Ridgmount Street, London WC1E 7AE, U.K.

Library Corporation, P.O. Box 40035, Washington, D.C. 20015, U.S.A.

Lotus Development Corporation, 55 Cambridge Parkway, Cambridge, MA 02142, U.S.A.

McGraw-Hill Book Company, 1221 Avenue of the Americas, New York, NY 10020, U.S.A.

Micromedex Inc., 660 Bannock Street, Denver, Colorado 80204, U.S.A.

Pergamon Infoline (Compact Solution), 12 Vandy Street, London, EC2A 2DE, U.K.

Postcodes, The Post Office, Headquarters Building, 33 Grosvenor Place, London SW1X 1PX, U.K.

Publishers Databases Ltd., c/o Mandarin Communications Ltd., Brettenham House, 5 Lancaster Place, London WC2E 7EN, U.K.

J. Whitaker & Sons Ltd., 12 Dyott Street, London WC1A 1DF, U.K.

REFERENCES

1. CD Data Report. Langley Publications Inc., 1350 Beverly Road, Suite 115-324, McLean, VA, U.S.A.

2. Optical Data Systems. Microinfo Ltd., P.O. Box 3, Newman Lane, Alton, Hants GU34 2PG, U.K.

3. Optical/Electronic Publishing Directory 1986. Learned Information, Woodside, Hinksey Hill, Oxford OX1 5AU, U.K.

10.   CONCLUSION - THE KEY ISSUES

In this report we have attempted to assess the potential impact of CD-ROM on the publishing and information industry and have compared CD-ROM with traditional paper, microfilm and online publishing systems.

Each chapter has dealt with a different aspect of CD-ROM systems and each has raised a number of important issues which need to be considered by anyone considering investing in CD-ROM systems, whether as a user or as a publisher. In this concluding chapter we want to highlight the key issues raised in each of the chapters and use them as the basis on which to make a few tentative predictions for the future.

In Chapters One and Seven we placed CD-ROM in context by comparing it with the other optical disk systems and by showing how it was related to them. The chief issue here was 'Will CD-ROM be usurped by some other optical publishing medium in future, are publishers who are moving into CD-ROM backing a long term successful product or is CD-ROM set to be superceded in the near future?'.

We concluded that, due to its standard format and use of proven technology, its basis in consumer CD systems, the widespread availability of CD mastering facilities and the potential for low cost volume production of the drives and media, CD-ROM looked likely to become the most attractive medium for distributing hundreds of copies of large textual and graphic databases to PC users. CD-ROM would be complemented by other read only media - such as hybrid videodiscs for handling mixed data and motion video and OROM/DataROM for high end multi-user applications - and not replaced by them.

In the second chapter we looked at existing CD-ROM standards and at developing standards, particularly the proposed High Sierra Group file format standard. The real issues here were: can standards ensure CD-ROM a future as a generic publishing medium accessible by most users of PCs and standard computer systems and how far can standards go before they constrain creative CD-ROM system designers, publishers and even the technology itself, given that higher density optical media will appear over the next few years? Clearly in many applications it will be desirable for end users who invest in CD-ROM hardware to be able to read a wide selection of discs on that hardware and to have some assurance that the hardware they have purchased will be usable over a 3 or 5 year period or however long they need to achieve a reasonable payback on their investment and we believe that the Philips and Sony Yellow Book standard plus the proposed High Sierra Group standard, provided it is widely adopted, will ensure that is the case.

Beyond that, however, one starts to look at how the data should be organised and indexed on the CD-ROM and hence what search software is needed to access it and it is clearly not practical or advisable to try and standardise indexing and retrieval software. The material placed on CD-ROM will differ considerably from application to application and the software needed to organise, index and access that data will also, inevitably, differ considerably to cater for the needs of specific categories of data and specific categories of end user. In many in-house and technical publishing applications, and even in many commercial publishing applications, CD-ROM systems will be sold to end users to do one specific job and they will want software designed for their specific requirements. Standards will not concern them at all.

One other area where standards, whether internationally agreed or imposed on a de facto basis by a dominant supplier, will be required in future is in the handling of mixed mode material. In many of the applications described in this report, mixed mode material (graphics and text on one page) will be handled. To make full use of the storage potential of CD-ROM and to provide users with faithful representations of original material, publishers will want to store the text in coded form and the graphics in vector or raster form and to retrieve and display them alongside each other just as currently is possible in desktop publishing systems. Before this is possible on a large scale using CD-ROM and standard PCs with high resolution screens, internationally agreed or de facto standards that define a page/document and its contents and how they are encoded, stored, transmitted and displayed, must be agreed and hence the work of ISO on Standard Generalised Markup Language and Office Document Architecture and the work of IBM in defining their own internal standards, are crucial here.

In the third chapter we looked at all the stages involved in the production of a CD-ROM product. The aim here was to stress that putting up to 200,000 pages of text on a CD-ROM, organising it and making it easily accessible via a standard PC is not a trivial task. Now that it is technically possible to produce a CD-ROM and now that there is agreement on a standard framework within which to operate, there is a need for software suppliers, system designers, data preparers and publishers to make considerable investments in designing CD-ROM products that do maximise the potential of CD-ROM. This includes developing and improving existing indexing and retrieval software, investigating how the material is formatted for display and redesigning user interfaces.

The other main issue raised in this chapter is the fact that currently, the infrastructure required to support major, time sensitive CD-ROM publishing ventures is still not fully established. The number of mastering and replication facilities currently offering CD-ROM services in Europe is limited and there are relatively few data preparers and system integrators. This situation will, no doubt, change over the next 12-18 months but currently there is not a great deal of choice for publishers wanting to deal with home based data preparation and mastering companies.

In the fourth chapter we looked at trends in workstation configurations and price. The key issues here are: how fast will the price come down, how compact will the units become and how standardised and stable is the whole PC world on which CD-ROM publishing is based?

Will we see vast reductions in price to the point where a CD-ROM workstation will be priced at a few hundred pounds or will the price stay at present levels? Currently, we are dealing with first generation modified consumer players which are not in mass production and are priced high due to the high value of the yen. As full and half-height CD-ROM drives become available and as sales volume increases so prices will come down steadily and if CD-ROM does become a high volume product, drive prices could drop to £200. However, CD-ROM is not a mainstream computer peripheral, it is a speciality product and the drive to lower prices must come from the drive suppliers and by publishers providing CD-ROM products which sell in high volume.

On the effect that changes in the design of PCs and PC operating systems will have on CD-ROM, nobody can predict this with certainty. Ideally, with CD-ROM we have defined a standard recording medium and a standard recording layout which allows data stored on CD-ROM to be read by PC users. As PCs become more powerful so users ought to be able to read data off the CD-ROMs more quickly and to be able to cater for high resolution graphics, video and audio. Provided the CD-ROM standard remains the same, the fact that the end user PCs may change should not present major problems. The alternative would be for dedicated publishing workstations to be developed - integrated units that combine CD-ROM drives and dedicated microprocessors - in the mould of the proposed CD-I standard player.

In the fifth chapter we looked at the wide range of potential application areas for CD-ROM, each one of which raises its own set of issues. Users working in each of these application areas are better equipped than we are to assess the potential of CD-ROM in their application, weighing up the factors described in Chapters One to Four, but a few general factors did emerge from this chapter.

Firstly, we have to define what is a realistic turnaround time for an updating CD-ROM based publishing service. Will it be financially and technically feasible to distribute parts catalogues on CD-ROM on a monthly basis? The indications are that it will be in future but it will require a very tight operation with the publisher investing heavily in the creation of a parts database that can be easily manipulated and updated on a regular basis and then output to CD-ROM following standard procedures.

Once the minimum turnaround time has been calculated, the next issue which will delay the introduction of CD-ROM distribution systems in in-house and technical publishing applications is what scale of investment is required to convert current page and image data into a form in which it can be easily handled, updated and output on CD-ROM.

If these two problem areas can be overcome then we feel the overall outlook for CD-ROM in in-house and technical publishing applications is good in the short to medium term. One of the main advantages here is that in-house users and many technical publishers will not worry unduly about software or hardware standards as they are dealing with a relatively controlled environment of branch offices or dealers and if CD-ROM proves more cost effective or more valuable than existing paper or microfilm distribution systems it will be installed without any need to consider other potential applications. However, CD-ROM will not have the entire market to itself. While CD-ROM will be used to distribute hundreds or even thousands of copies of technical manuals, where only a few tens of copies are required or where very fast turnaround times are required or security is a major factor, 5.25 inch WORM disks will be preferred.

Moving on to the specific applications which we identified in Chapter Five, we consider that in the first two - distributing software, documentation and graphic databases to computer users - CD-ROM will eventually find itself in competition with higher specification OROM/DataROM products and that at this stage it appears as if CD-ROM will be targeted at single user PC systems while OROM/DataROM products will be distributed to users of more powerful multi-user micro, mini and even mainframe users and users of specialised CAD systems, scientific workstations and electronic publishing systems.

Turning to commercial database publishing and the provision of specialised information services on CD-ROM, here we feel that the future is bright provided some of the issues raised in Chapter Five can be overcome. For database publishing the key issue is an economic one: how to make information available on CD-ROM at a price that does not undermine existing online revenues and, indeed, how to combine backfile distribution on CD-ROM with online access to the most recent data. For new, end-user oriented specialist information services on CD-ROM the key issue would be how to make the entire database, which would undoubtedly include text and both vector and raster graphics, easily accessible by end users with simple, helpful user interfaces.

Looking at backfile/collection distribution, we made the point that it would be many years before CD-ROM could compete with microfilm as a way of distributing large collections of old books or backruns of journals to libraries and other corporate users.

It will not prove economic to distribute raster scanned images of document pages on CD-ROM in high volume but if, as mentioned above, standards for dealing with mixed mode documents are agreed and the journal publishers can deliver their text in coded form and the graphics in raster form then the storage capacities of CD-ROM would change dramatically and the economics of CD-ROM for distributing backfiles of journals and large full text collections would become very attractive.

Looking at the library marketplace we felt that there was a considerable market for bibliographic databases on CD-ROM for staff use but there are several unresolved issues concerning the use of CD-ROM systems by library patrons. The first is that libraries would need to invest in large numbers of CD-ROM workstations and hence will wait until costs come down. The second is that many of the CD-ROM products will not be quick reference type material and hence users will want to spend longer on the terminals than economics will allow. The third is the question of supervision of hardware and valuable software and the fourth is the high subscription cost to CD-ROM products.

Moving on to the educational and consumer marketplace we found so many unresolved issues and so many possible competitors to CD-ROM and CD-I products that it was extremely difficult to make any detailed predictions except that we feel the marketplace will prove more difficult to crack than the corporate, database and technical publishing markets described above. As with videodiscs, the main issue will revolve around overcoming the vicious circle of a lack of high quality software leading to depressed hardware sales and a low installed base which in turn deters software providers from investing in CD-ROM and CD-I.

In Chapter Six we then went on to compare CD-ROM with traditional paper, microfilm and online distribution systems. The general findings were that CD-ROM will be best suited to the distribution of large volumes of mixed mode - textual and graphic - information to large numbers of PC users who have a requirement to access the information in a range of different ways and to download sub-sets of that data for subsequent processing on their own PCs. CD-ROM would not compete with online systems for distributing volatile information, it would not compete with microfilm in the near future for the distribution of high volumes of relatively low use material and it would not compete with paper for the distribution of small amounts of material to a wide range of different users.

Chapter Seven compared CD-ROM with other optical publishing media and reinforced the findings of Chapter One.

Chapter Eight listed the main CD-ROM drive suppliers, data preparers and system integrators and reinforced the conclusions of Chapter Three that the required infrastructure for serious CD-ROM publishing applications is still developing in Europe.

Chapter Nine looked at the other side of the coin, listing some of the companies who have announced and shown commercial CD-ROM products. The list is considerably shorter than the list of companies experimenting with CD-ROM, again emphasising that we are still in the early stages of development and many publishers are still very uncertain about the way in which the industry will develop and how they should position themseleves within it.

Overall, therefore, there are still many unresolved issues but considerable progress has been made over the past two years and there are far fewer people today than two years ago who are prepared to write CD-ROM off as a publishing medium. The question really is how quickly will the momentum build up and will the entry cost and the cost of hardware seriously restrict the potential market for CD-ROM services or will CD-ROM grow steadily over the years until it truly becomes a generic publishing medium and a generally accepted alternative to paper, microfilm and online distribution systems?

We believe, after researching for this report, that the truth inevitably lies somewhere between these two positions. CD-ROM will prove itself to be a long term publishing medium for PC users but it will find itself bounded by, on the one hand, the demand from mainstream computer users for higher performance multi-user systems and, on the other hand, the demand from schools, libraries and domestic users for lower cost hardware and software. The first demand may well be met long term by OROM or DataROM systems and the latter demand will be met by dedicated systems such as CD-I.

Exactly how large the CD-ROM window is, is difficult to predict but our feeling is that it is not as large as many of the market survey companies are predicting. 1985 was the year of announcements and 'vapourware'; 1986 has been the year of demonstrations and a few successful products; 1987 will see a number of niche markets developing, particularly technical publishing and in-house applications; 1988 will be the first real boom year when database publishing, special information systems and reference publishing on CD-ROM really takes off and 1989/90 will see the start of serious moves in the domestic consumer and educational marketplaces.

The experts have predicted that by 1990 we will see anything from a conservative 1 million up to a staggering 22 million CD-ROM/CD-I drives installed. We would tend to support the findings of market research company Freeman Associates who predict that by 1991 some 440,000 CD-ROM drives will be selling each year at a market value of approximately $154 million. To them this is a relatively small marketplace when compared to the market for WORM disk drives which they expect to be worth $1,488 billion in 1991.

Small or not in computer terms, if 440,000 PC users are buying CD-ROM drives each year by 1991 then the market for CD-ROM publishing will be very bouyant indeed and many of the publishers going through the painful process of designing and producing CD-ROM products can be assured of getting a good payback on their investment.